To the clever and beautiful Chris,
Hey! I found my voice
Susie xx

PUBLISHED IN THE UK BY
THE FOODTALK GROUP

SWIMMING ON MY OWN
(THE BUSINESS CASE FOR KINDNESS AND EQUALITY)

ISBN 978-1-7397894-0-4

GW00660180

1

Born into inner city poverty against a backdrop of racist and misogynistic 1960s Britain, Susie finally 'made it' becoming a self-made multi-millionaire at 58 years old. Admittedly slower than some entrepreneurs, but she got there in the end.

Sick of working for bullies and misogynists she decided to set up her own company with her best friend's daughter, Brady Last. They started in her small conservatory on two laptops and with a large stash of Yorkshire tea bags. The kids had left home so she thought she should do something risky for once in her life.

She put her entire savings into starting a business even though there were no clients in sight. Susie wanted her own brand, one that had design and her quirky humour at its heart. She wanted to create a company culture based on respect and kindness and managed to convince Brady to join her in this one last hurrah.

Competitors laughed at them, banks wouldn't give them an overdraft (never mind a loan), and rivals tried to put them out of business. Five years later it was sold in a multi-million pound deal to a blue chip multinational. How did she build a buy-out in such a short time and from scratch?

Susie has made waves as a woman in business, and here she sets out the things she learnt along the way and with a bit of luck, if she can do it, why can't you?

To Kate and JoJo, the two most beautiful,
funny and clever women in my world
and to Simon who made me truly happy again.

CONTENTS

CHAPTER 1
Taking the plunge

**"Don't wait for
your ship to come
in – swim out to it."**

Steve Southerland

This book is dedicated to every kind and thoughtful person out there who is trying to juggle work and home and struggling to find a balance. I salute you.

I was going to write this anonymously because I was afraid of the abuse I would get and the people I might upset. But I think that rather defeats the object. My birth name is Susan Griffiths, but I was Sue Nelson for 34 years. I'm not a child, although I was often made to feel like one by bullies in my workplace, social circle and home life. After decades of keeping quiet and keeping things to myself, I've decided to exchange the safety of silence for the highly vulnerable position of speaking out about how the world of business is unbelievably biased.

I think I had huge potential even from the beginning, but I often squandered it by allowing myself to be held back. I was complicit in it, but in my defence the inequality and bullying was so overwhelming that I usually retreated into being passive and accommodating.

All that changed in 2016 when, at 54 years old, I finally ran out of patience, or maybe I just got brave. I really didn't care anymore because my career was practically over, so was my marriage, I had nothing to lose. My hair was grey (although carefully coloured) and my wrinkles deep. That's when you're dangerous, because if you don't care, no one has any leverage over you.

Four things happened that made me decide to write this book. First it was the #metoo movement, secondly there was Donald Trump, third I became rather wealthy after selling my business and later, there was the tragic murder of Sarah Everard. I want to explain that even though others might lie, cheat, steal and terrorise their way to the top, nice people don't necessarily come last or succumb to a terrible fate. We can succeed too.

#metoo hit a chord for me, but only because it was how I was starting to think anyway. It's not a rallying cry that I joined. Contrary to media opinion it's not a group or a campaign either. You won't find me getting a #metoo tattoo, or any tattoo for that matter because my mum told me they're common.

'Women's Day of Action', Miami

When it surfaced it was such a relief to know that I wasn't the only one who'd suffered sexual harassment and the constant background hum of misogyny for years and years and years. Not just socially but in business. Crucially, I started to think that maybe it wasn't something I'd brought on myself, there were others. Not hundreds of them but millions. I also felt the need to explain that despite setbacks, making very big mistakes and outrageous bias you can still make it, even when facing unwarranted aggression, misogyny, racism, ageism and/or homophobia.

'Women Against Sexual Harassment', Rome

I wanted to speak out for people that usually don't have a voice. Those of us who keep quiet, both male and female, because we're not as well educated, or privileged or we're shy or just intimidated by what is sometimes described as the 'alpha males' that disproportionately occupy key positions in our society. They're powerful but I'm going to be brave because too often they get there by being utter bastards and it's not right. I've called them out in this book and I think I have shown that their behaviour just doesn't fit the modern world anymore and in the long term it too often goes disastrously wrong.

I managed to create a business from scratch without any help and sell it just five years later to a multi-billion pound international company. I think I did it with kindness and with a great respect for true equality. I've learnt so much along the way and also made some howling mistakes but I believe it's proved that good people can succeed. Given all that experience it seems such a waste not to share it because I hope, just hope it might help other entrepreneurs, especially those where it's not quite working out just now.

Finally, I'm not anti-male or believe that women are totally virtuous and can't be bullies too. Of course not. It's just that I heard Jude Kelly* say once that we need a new set of stories to describe what inequality <u>feels</u> like, not what it looks like, so I thought . . . well, here's one for you.

* Judith Kelly CBE, Artistic Director of the Southbank Centre in London and Founder of Women of the World Festival speaking at the Change Makers 2018 event at Bloomberg, London 24 April.

CHAPTER 2
Bikini ready

**"It doesn't matter who you are,
where you come from.
The ability to triumph
begins with you — always."**

Oprah Winfrey

I was born in inner city London in 1961. That year the E-type Jaguar was launched, JF Kennedy was president and all tv programmes (if you were among the elite that had a telly) were in black and white. It was also the year the contraceptive pill was made available. This hugely important social development allowed women to take control of their sex lives and when they had children. Men entering their teens and early twenties were surrounded by the mantra of 'free' love and single women who need not get pregnant. This had never happened before. It was the 'swinging sixties' and the media urged everyone to take part. Rising wages and full employment meant that, especially if you were a man, you could move jobs anytime you felt like it because your skills and experience were desperately needed. This gives you a particular mindset.

Martin Luther King Jr has a dream in 1963

In my early primary school years, The Beatles, Bob Dylan and Jimi Hendrix were writing the best songs, Marilyn Monroe was a sex symbol and Neil Armstrong stepped on the moon. *To Kill A Mockingbird* was published and *Psycho* was released. But despite the 'make love not war' slogans it was a time of global violence. JFK and Robert F Kennedy were assassinated, as was Martin Luther King. Mods and rockers were viciously clashing. There was dreadful bloodshed in Vietnam and mass public riots in France.

JFK just before his assassination

The Lady Chatterley trial begun. Apparently, it was outrageous to print a book (even though it was written by D.H. Lawrence decades before), that claimed orgasms could be had by women and that sex might be fun. Viv Nicholson won the football pools (if you're under 50 look up 'football pools' on Wikipedia) vowing to 'spend, spend, spend'. The Moors murders hit the headlines with the police photo of Myra Hindley seared on our brains. And although society was becoming more tolerant, Mary Whitehouse waged war on the dangerous liberals exposing the public to 'smut' and, god-forbid, homosexuals in broad daylight (LGBTQ+ community look away).

Against this backdrop I was born in Annie McCall's nursing home in Clapham, south London. My Mum was 22 years old. Annie McCall was one of the first 50 female doctors and her specialism was midwifery. She set up an all-woman hospital staffed by female doctors and nurses. It was truly revolutionary at the time. The hospital took in poor women and those having children out of wedlock (as it was called then). She focussed on superior healthcare and hygiene. McCall died in 1949 but the hospital continued until 1970.

For the first year of my life my parents lived in a flat with no running water. I don't quite know how my mum coped with no available water in the house with a newborn baby, maybe that's why my immune system is so good. Today, millennials grumble that they may never own their own home, but then I didn't know anyone who did or even dream that they might.

My dad was one of eight and my mum was one of three. When my mum was a toddler at the start of the Second World War she was looked after relatives because my maternal grandmother, Winnifred Manns, had polio and was unable to speak and walk for two years. Win's whole family including her mum and sister were killed around that time in a direct hit on an underground shelter where they were hiding from a German air raid.

My maternal grandfather, Harry, was in prison for robbery for a while which made one of my favourite album's *Strangeways Here We Come* all the more apt later on. Being banged up in HM Prison Manchester, my Mum and her sisters were brought up by a lone parent for two years, one that had only just recovered from polio and whose immediate family had been obliterated. Harry's dad was killed in the First World War when he was a very young child, just one week before Germany signed the armistice to end the conflict in 1918.

My other grandmother, Florence Griffiths, lost her husband early on. He started work at 12 as a labourer and died of a heart attack before he was 50 years old. Her father was killed in the First World War too, so as the eldest she jointly brought up her siblings with her mum, who was illiterate. I always remember Nanny Griff as grumpy and humourless, but I guess you would be if you started life like that and then had eight kids of your own, two having died before school age. Nearly every family from whatever class would have similar stories of family tragedies scarred by the two world wars.

I really loved Win, my 'nanny Manns' as I called her. I still miss her. She gave birth to my mum at 18 and so when I was born she was only 40 years old. She was a young grandma and was always ready to laugh and have fun despite her circumstances. I didn't feel the same attachment to the very dour Nanny Griff who was 22 years older. She was literally from another generation.

Win and Harry, when he was not in prison, lived in a tiny downstairs flat in Willesden, north west London with an outside toilet and no bathroom. Upstairs lived Rube (Ruby) and Jack. They didn't have children, which seemed odd at the time, or any teeth. I think it was the thing then to have all your teeth pulled out and a set of pearly white false ones installed instead. I have no idea why. They rarely put their teeth in, except on special occasions or to eat something that needed chewing.

Nanny Manns aged 19 with my Mum

We'd often visit nanny Manns on a weekend. She made a fabulous Sunday lunch with her roast potatoes the crowning glory. Grandad was a painter and decorator when he wasn't nicking stuff. So we used to have a pasting table set up in the living room with a tablecloth on top and odd different height chairs gathered around it. It was always the best meal of the week. My brother and I would get sent upstairs to see Rube and Jack an hour before serving to get us out of the way. They would be preparing their roast too, but they ate much later so we would chat while Rube 'poked her greens' and peeled the potatoes. Essentially, she cooked cabbage (greens) for an exceedingly long time and would periodically poke them for some reason which I've never understood. The smell still haunts me.

My dad Les with a full ashtray

Jack was a lorry driver and part-time fence for stolen property. His flat was always stuffed with ill-gotten gains he was trying to flog. He took a real shine to me and would often bring out something for me to keep or give to my mum. Once he gave me a watch, which I still remember. It was gold (not real obviously) and turquoise. I was so proud of it, not realising that it had once belonged to someone else, and he had no right to own it or pass it on.

They had a bar with optics in their 'front room' which wouldn't have been out of place in Nelson Mandela House in *Only Fools and Horses*. Next to it was a rather tatty piano. We felt so grown up as we sat on a bar stool and got served a snowball with a cocktail cherry while Rube gave the old Joanna a bashing and sang traditional cockney songs. I would've been at primary school then, but they thought it perfectly normal to serve us a drink of egg yolks, sugar, brandy and vanilla at midday and before you'd hit your teenage years. When we left them to go downstairs and tuck into our Sunday lunch, they would give the greens a final poke, put their gnashers in, dish up and then get fabulously drunk.

After lunch, me and my brother would sit on the backyard wall and throw stones at the rats scampering around in the derelict house next door. It was good to have some outside space albeit tiny, because most people we knew didn't have that luxury. In the backyard there was a tin bath hung on a nail on the wall. This wasn't unusual. Basically, you filled it up once a week in front of an electric bar fire in the living room and that's how you got clean. Not very private and probably not very safe either. Other than that, you had what my mum called a 'strip down wash' or when you were very young just had a bath in the sink with the ascot dangling over, leaning forward so your back didn't come into contact with the blue gas flame.

Everyone I mixed with had the same upbringing and circumstances. We had an outside toilet and no bathroom and so did all my aunts, uncles and grandparents. I'd never heard of anyone having a shower and had never seen one, except at the municipal swimming baths or on campsites. When I left home many years later and my grandparents had moved, I asked my nan what happened to Rube and Jack. She replied that Jack had died and Rube **"had her leg off"** which translated means amputated. Basically by then, not only had her teeth gone missing but so had her husband and one of her legs too.

I had lots of relations to mix with as I had 18 aunts and uncles and too many cousins to mention, but one was my particular favourite - aunty Stevie. She was my mum's younger sister and was only 12 years older than me. She'd been expelled from school which was quite an achievement in those days, god knows what she'd done. She got pregnant and had to get married at 17, as you were expected to do then. My brother and I used to go and stay with her for two weeks in the summer holidays because her husband had left her and disappeared off the face of the planet. I was dispatched to sort of help out and keep her company. I loved it. She had no rules, unlike my parents who were very strict. We didn't have to brush our teeth or hair, have a bath or even a wash and neither did we have a set bedtime. I was 11 years old, my brother two years younger and my two cousins Robin and Jason were seven and two.

Stevie would do cleaning jobs during the day to make ends meet. When she got back, we would cook, watch the black and white telly that had to be fed with 50p pieces in a slot at the back and then stay up until 3am playing three-card brag.

We bet all our pocket money on these card games. She won each time which I guess was a way of getting coins to feed the telly. I would therefore be responsible for three children during the day, with one still in nappies.   Periodically I would take the pram with all our washing down to the launderette in the local shopping precinct.

While the wash was on, I would take everyone to the newsagents to buy some sweets for lunch and two packets of Players No 6 cigarettes for my aunt. Then you could buy cigarettes as a child if you had a note from a grown up. Afterwards we'd traipse back home with the cleaned and dry washing and the four of us would wait for her to get in to make dinner. I shudder when I look back and think of all the things that could have gone wrong. I'm certain my mum and dad had no clue as to how we spent those annual fortnights, but we kept quiet because it was the high point of our school holiday each year.

Although Stevie's husband had buggered off and couldn't be found even by the Salvation Army, not one of my family had been divorced and yet many of those marriages weren't exactly idyllic.

My mum worked as a shop assistant in Regent Street, got married at 19 to my dad, a manual worker, and they stayed married until he died in 2007. He got a scholarship to grammar school but was never allowed to go because his mum forced him out to earn money. Years later in the factory where he worked, he would do *The Telegraph* crossword at lunchtime in the canteen, and I don't remember a single evening when he didn't have his nose i n a book.

I went to Macaulay School in Clapham, which was a mixed-race school full of kids from the local area and children of the newly arrived Windrush immigrants who were needed to fill the labour shortage. Mostly everybody was poor at the school and violence was commonplace. I got beaten up in my first week as a five-year-old. This was my first taste of being bullied. It was a shock because I couldn't work out what I'd done to deserve it. I wasn't hurt badly, but quite a bit of blood. I didn't get much sympathy from my parents. My mum was pretty irritated because it meant she had to wash the blood off my uniform and have it ready for the next morning. I found all this perplexing. If I hadn't done anything wrong, why would someone hit me? And if someone hurt me why would my parents not sympathise?

Me in my Sunday best clothes and
with my National Health glasses

The kids in my local school, 1967

The attitude was to get on with it and don't cry or complain. I think that's because such families have a myriad of problems that make getting through the day hard enough, and you having a bruised and bloodied nose is not rated too highly up there. I probably got beaten up because I was small for my age and, with a pronounced squint and poor eyesight, had to wear a patch on one eye and thick National Health glasses. I was an easy target in a school where fighting in the playground was seen as a good way to let off steam. The patch eventually went (weird that I would later marry someone called Nelson), and I learnt two very important lessons; get people to like you and they won't physically hurt you and if they do, learn not to say anything.

I stuck to this for decades, which on reflection was not a very healthy strategy.

The late 1960s and 1970s was a turbulent time in inner city London, in particular the focus on race. There were street battles with the National Front and other neo-nazi groups, violence at the Notting Hill Carnival and later around the corner from where we lived, the Brixton riots.

Outwardly racist tv programmes like *Love Thy Neighbour* would commonly refer to black people as nignogs and sambo (it makes me wince just typing those words). *It Ain't Half Hot Mum* was a popular programme supposedly based in India that made jokes about Indians, Burmese and Japanese people, with white men always in a position of authority and superiority. This was a reflection of reality of course, not just in India during the war but in Britain in the 70s.

Although racism was rife, and this permeated my consciousness, I also felt very strongly that racism and racist comments were wrong. I don't know where I got this from. It might be because I went to a multi-racial school and what I saw didn't match the portrayal on tv. It might have been that some of my school friends were black and Asian and they seemed perfectly normal to me. It could also be that racism inflamed my ridiculously strong sense of fairness and dislike of bullying behaviour. Anyhow, notably at this time, I didn't perceive any overt misogyny or sexism.

I passed the 11+ and we moved to Kent. I started at an all girls' grammar school. Grandmother Flo refused to speak to me after that because it was a betrayal of our working-class roots and she thought I would have ideas above my station. There is such a thing as inverted snobbery.

This period was the late 1970s to early 1980s. By this time sexist behaviour and attitudes to women and girls had pierced my consciousness. Popular culture was fiercely misogynistic and I had started to notice, but given my fondness for fair play my reaction to it was really quite odd.

For example, Michael Parkinson whose interview programmes were hugely admired and influential then, gave a famous interview with Helen Mirren, now Dame Helen Mirren, asking if her big bosoms would detract from her acting performances. Nobody remotely turned a hair at that question except Helen. She objected and was severely castigated for being a difficult interviewee. I'm certain that would have affected her early career.

I thought she was being difficult too and that her aggressive and indignant response was wrong. Women didn't do that. She must've been 'a feminist' and that wasn't culturally acceptable. Parkinson was revered and I wasn't often allowed to stay up late and watch his programmes, but it was clear to me that he came out as the winner. We all loved Parky.

The Benny Hill Show was big on tv too. It won multiple awards and at its peak was watched by 21 million viewers. Smiley Benny played the middle-aged lead character convincingly. Essentially, he was a predatory and creepy sex pest who would leer and chase after women. For some unfathomable reason they would run around British streets in their bikinis chased by Hill who was often dressed as a milkman. I know?!

Stringfellows was launched in Covent Garden by Peter Stringfellow around the same time. It was symptomatic of the cultural vibe and became a phenomenal success. He knew how to capitalise on the zeitgeist - the era of perpetually ogling female bodies with a lecherous running

A typical photoshoot for *The Benny Hill Show*

commentary. I didn't really think there was anything wrong with these attitudes that surrounded me. It just made me conscious that I needed to work on my body and make it 'bikini ready' if I wanted men to chase me. I dieted a lot, but that bikini body never happened until I was so old it didn't matter.

I was 16 when the biggest film for some time was launched. In 1977, *Saturday Night Fever* had a soundtrack by the Bee Gees with John Travolta as the lead character. We all thought he was the epitome of cool. In the film he seduced his girlfriend by trying to rape her in the back seat of a car.

A typical photoshoot involving Peter Stringfellow

Nobody commented and nobody seemed to think that was wrong. I thought she was lucky to be the subject of John Travolta's attention.

I wasn't academically intelligent enough to go to university, or so my teachers told me. In those days less than 5 percent of school leavers went to uni although now it's more like 50 percent. It was pretty difficult then to be working class with no family support or parental experience of such things to get into higher education. The standard career advice if you were a girl and smart enough to go to grammar school but not clever enough to get a degree, was to be a teacher or a nurse. There didn't appear to be any other options.

I didn't fancy teaching difficult kids and I have absolutely no sympathy or empathy for anyone that's ill, so I didn't think

I'd make a very good nurse. If you were middle class and couldn't get into university, you could be a secretary and get trained at one of the posh secretarial colleges like the Lucy Clayton Charm Academy (yes, that was a real place). Apparently, they taught you things like shorthand and how to get out of a low sports car without flashing your knickers. I definitely was too bright and too working class to get in through those hallowed doors.

My parents and grandparents clearly had tough and difficult lives with no prospect of them getting better. I wanted to transcend that. Break out of it. But given my background what should I do? What could I do?

Me at 16 and John Travolta in the same year

CHAPTER 3
Sharks in the pool

"I don't even know who I would have said anything to. It was just the kind of thing you put up with."

Nicola Sturgeon

Education seemed to be the answer. I would get educated and then would come a good job. Trouble was I wasn't classically academic or able to fall back on family connections. I could draw though, so I went to art college working my way through with cleaning and bar jobs as my parents didn't have any money to support me. My bar work meant I had to endure the most awful comments about my sexual availability, the visual condition of my body, particularly the size of my bum and boobs. All openly discussed. You were fair game to be judged and leered at, often in very loud conversation, or (my favourite) suffer individual comments from sad blokes sitting on bar stools for hours, unashamedly watching your every move. It was just normal.

One guy (I was 18 he was probably 40) used to grope me every week when I cleared tables. Him and his pals were always the last to leave. I was so sick of being touched and having to wait well past closing time to get rid of them, that one day when I was particularly tired and they refused to leave the bar, I poured the remains of his beer over his head. There wasn't a lot of it, but he did get a soaking. He complained to the male manager of the bar and I lost my job. What he'd done and said wasn't taken into account. What I did was the only thing that was considered. You may say it was stupid of me not to try and find some way to ask them all to desist, but I knew it would antagonise them and make it worse.

At this time too, it was absolutely accepted that you got paid less than men even if you had the same job. It was also customary that you would face rampant sexism and discrimination at every turn if you wanted to get on. It wasn't mentioned, you didn't complain, it was just how it was. My outward tactic both professionally and socially was pretty much the same as every other woman I knew, which was to avoid confrontation if at all possible. Less trouble, less aggression, less energy-sapping and less upsetting.

As a single female student, I know this is a sickening thing to say, but sometimes I had sex to be polite because otherwise it would result in an argument which I hated, or worse, put you in a position of physical danger. So, it's true to say that sometimes I said yes for expediency and good manners. I didn't sleep around a lot at all, because I was reasonably shy and lacking in physical confidence, but it seemed that contraception and sexual freedom was giving guys a great time but I'm not so sure I was. In that respect I have felt like Margot in Kristen Roupenian's *Cat Person* and wondered what the hell I did it for? The guys I met seemed intent on their own sexual gratification but not mine.

In terms of both physical power, status and influence I was weaker and men knew it. But then again so did I. That's how you felt most of the time; at a disadvantage, always vulnerable and a tiny bit afraid. Margaret Atwood is widely quoted as saying that: **"Men are afraid that women will laugh at them. Women are afraid that men will kill them."** It's not far from the truth.

Ministry of Justice statistics for 2019* show that women make up just 4 percent of the prison population, with the most likely crimes being shoplifting or drug offences. Consequently, 73 percent are serving one year or less and just under half are there because their offence was to support someone else's drug use. It's roughly the same level for the rest of the western world. In essence, violent crime is a male pastime with studies consistently showing that only 18 percent of women are in prison for violent acts, way less than men. When you're leaving a building and there's no one around, or you're walking to your car in a spooky municipal car park or it's dark and you're on your own, it's a legitimate concern that if there's a man around, they might hurt or kill you.

As Grayson Perry puts it in his book *Descent of Man*: **"Most violent people, rapists, criminals, killers, tax avoiders, corrupt politicians, planet despoilers, sex abusers and dinner-party bores, do tend to be, well… men."**

My experience of early adult single life from 18 to 22 as a student with part-time poorly paid work, was that men would take advantage of me in one way or another whether to the detriment of my work, my social standing or my physical wellbeing. The complete and utter norm was to be shouted at with sordid comments when you walked past a building site, groped on the tube or in other crowded situations and that this would happen at least every week if not most days.

It's honestly true that most women my age have been flashed at and had to endure some bloke masturbating in front of them and this was usually when you were alone in a public place or walking home at night. During such occasions you were supposed to either ignore it, say something witty but not aggressive, or simply run away. This doesn't even cover the bullying I encountered at work. Nicola Sturgeon, First Minister of Scotland who seems to me to be highly driven and unlikely to put up with too much crap, has talked about her early career. In a 2020 interview with a *Sunday Times* journalist she admitted:

"The thing about #MeToo is it has made a lot of people, me included, reassess things that at the time you just put up with. You know, guys kind of

touching you in slightly uncomfortable ways, and the leering. I remember having lunch in my early twenties with a guy who was the political editor of a big Scottish newspaper at the time, and the whole conversation was kind of conducted at this level (she gestures to her bust) **and it just felt really uncomfortable."** She said nothing to him or anyone at the time. Because it seemed normal to her? **"Yeah. And I guess he probably didn't think he was doing anything particularly untoward. I don't even know who I would have said anything to. It was just the kind of thing you put up with."**

The Crime Survey for England and Wales estimated that more than 618,000 women experienced at least one sexual assault involving rape, attempted rape, indecent exposure or unwanted touching in a year (April 2019 to March 2020). The largest segment who had been assaulted were those aged between 10 and 14 years old. An investigation in 2021 by UN Women UK found that 97 percent of women aged 18-24 have been sexually harassed, and a further 96 percent not reporting those situations because of the belief that it would not change anything.

Figures vary but it seems that less than 4 percent of men have ever experienced sexual assault in their entire adult lives. It's obvious that a man is unlikely to know how this fear of crime feels. They simply don't know that women walk around all day wary that in some situations they might get hurt. I guess it's not a man's fault to have no understanding of how this feels it's just that he will have no concept of it.

This is clearly demonstrated by the quote from the fashion designer Oscar de la Renta aimed at women presumably wearing his designer wear: **"Walk like you have three men walking behind you."** When this was published recently on *Buzzfeed*, lots of women had never heard or seen it before. This is the overall gist of the reaction to it:

"It genuinely took me a minute to realize this meant 'walk sexy so they stare at your ass' and not 'walk quickly and/or run because you are in danger'. Men are so fucking stupid and have zero conception of what being a woman in public is actually like."

"So I'd be pretending I'm on the phone and dropping hints that I'm a judo instructor. Is that how I am supposed to walk, Oscar? Because that's what I do when three men are following me at night. I also start speed walking. Goddammit Oscar, do you have any idea what it's like being a woman walking alone?? Do you???"

"Every single woman who read (sic) **this immediately think** (sic)**, 'Walk faster. Change directions. Surround yourself with people. Call your mom/sister/friend. Tell her where you are.'"**

Even though there can be a loud debate on social media about the topic, female victims don't generally report their experience to the police, so it's not just me. Sexual assault (as opposed to rape) was treated in conversation as something that was funny all those years ago even if at the time it made you feel very threatened. Your women friends wouldn't console you as if it was something unpleasant. You were expected to be flattered and laugh at it.

So, the truth is, if any of this happened, women would not

side with you and men didn't comprehend that it was not warranted or welcomed or even that it might be a problem. All of the data we have now, reflected my experience as a student. Without much family support (get on with it) or a culture where you didn't talk about such things (get on with it), it made me feel lonely inside school and college. Somehow I was an outsider and I didn't fit anywhere.

* England and Wales. In 2017 it was reported that almost 40 percent of those women had previously attempted suicide and 48 percent had suffered domestic violence. Two thirds are mothers with children under 18.

CHAPTER 4
Holding my breath

**"Women stay with abusive
partners for all kinds of
reasons – they love them,
they fear them, they have children
with them, they believe they
can change them or they
simply have nowhere else to go."**

Kate Thornton

Then, I met my husband when I was 22. I lived with him for 32 years. He was 30 and I was the ideal woman age (more of which later) when we met. I was plain Jane. A penniless student, slightly on the outside of everything, not really fitting anywhere. He had a good job, a sports car and a house. He was the life and soul of the party and he always seemed like he 'belonged' right in the middle of a social crowd or at work. He was undoubtedly the most handsome man I had ever met. I couldn't believe he could be interested in someone like me.

Me at 22 years old . . .

. . . and madly, deeply in love

What I didn't know was this good-looking, charismatic bon
viveur was seriously damaged underneath it all. He
physically hurt me and verbally abused me, but he didn't
mean to. I'm terribly ashamed to announce that, I suppose
I let him and didn't tell anyone or do anything about it. He
loved me very deeply but was an alcoholic and in private
threatened to kill himself on many occasions. I allowed
him to function. I made that possible. Perhaps if I hadn't,
he would have got the help that, I can see so clearly now,
he needed. But I was so in love. Despite his behaviour we

got married and soon had two beautiful children. Maybe I thought I could change him, heal him or he would grow out of it.

I feel guilty about my approach, but for the sake of harmony and keeping our two young girls inside a stable family, I took it on the chin and made sure that outwardly everything looked idyllic and stable. Marriage was a must then. You had to find a husband. If not, you didn't really have a place in society. There wasn't anywhere for you to fit. You were going to be lonely and financial survival would be very tough indeed. I would be outside again.

As part of this deal, my husband (mostly) made sure that any arguments or worse never happened in front of the children or anyone else. He may have been a rubbish husband on occasions, but he was actually a very good dad when the children were young. It is possible to be these two things at once.

To me, my two polarised options would be 1) to put up with it or 2) leave. I didn't consider discussion, counselling or anything else like that as a possibility. Apparently, counselling was for people that were mentally ill (stigmatised then) or didn't have friends. Anyhow, this would most definitely lead to an argument that was likely to result in violence or severe, verbally threatening abuse or he might carry out one of his many threats to kill himself. If you don't argue you don't get hurt and importantly nor does anyone else.

When my husband was sober, he was funny, romantic, flattering and he made me feel amazing, so I just waited for those days. I loved him deeply when he was like that and such days came along reasonably often enough to make you hang on and wait for the next one. As Margaret Atwood wrote somewhere: **"When we think of the past it's the beautiful things we pick out. We want to believe it was all like that."**

Leaving was a nuclear option anyhow. To me it meant that my two daughters would gain another mother and I absolutely didn't want to share them with anyone else. I cannot state emphatically enough that I thought they would get really messed up if I ceded control, and their destiny and their characters would be less rounded and robust in order to take on the world as discriminated females. In one way very selfish and arrogant, and in another, selfless and naïve.

I'm not overstating my particular abilities as a mum, that's not the point. I just believed that if the family was fractured it would, by its nature, make them more confused and vulnerable, less equipped to have a happy and fulfilling life later on and less able to deal with their Dad if he was with another partner who couldn't or wouldn't shield them from his behaviour. So that was my top priority - bringing them up without familial complications or interference from someone with different values from me. Yes, I was being selfish.

Socially speaking if I left, not that I had the money, it would make me a woman with no man and a single mother. This was seen as a very bad thing. Pariah status could ensue. It would involve a lengthy, bruising battle over finances, visiting rights and living accommodation. It would also mean the children would find out that their brilliant dad was coincidentally an intermittently monstrous husband.

I always wanted for them to have a great relationship with their dad and not side with either party. To me, our relationship with each other was far less important than their

43

relationship with the two of us. I kept all this from my children until they left home a couple of years ago, and then I did too.

I left with just my clothes and nothing else after 32 years. My husband was prone to irrational drunken behaviour and had guns in the house, so I didn't tell anyone where I was living (even my children) just to make sure I was safe. I was terrified that if he didn't hurt me then he might hurt himself. But I just thought I would have to live with the guilt if it did happen. He threatened it often enough, but I was so unhappy by then I was banking on it being a weird type of control mechanism and hoped that through all those years he was actually bluffing.

I hired a holiday home which was fully kitted out, (I didn't even have a knife and fork), because by this time I could afford to do so. It would have taken much more courage to leave if I didn't have access to a salary and a good few months' worth of money to see me through the first stage of financial arguments and hysterically aggressive email and text abuse. All the time I kept working and running my business, without a hint of what was happening to anyone else.

Even now, other women in the same position just can't get out because of their financial situation. The most recent YouGov data shows that many women rely on their partner to get by financially, even if they work full-time themselves. Among men it's much rarer. 35 percent of all women with a partner are either "entirely" or "somewhat" dependent on their other half. This is only true for 11 percent of men with a spouse or permanent partner, including just 3 percent who are completely reliant on the other.

Lots of women are like me in that they endure a situation for literally decades. They construct an environment and unwritten set of operating rules that creates the maximum amount of harmony possible, even though keeping up the illusion means you're living on a knife edge all the time. In any case it didn't happen every day, just occasionally, and so you could con yourself into thinking that the most recent abuse would be the last especially when the in-between times could be pretty good.

This has happened to more friends my age than I thought possible. Perhaps ours was the first financially independent and well-educated generation of wives who, when their children left home, didn't have to put up with all that shit. Most especially when we earned the same or more, than our supposedly smarter husbands whose careers inexplicably came before ours. We all share the same trait – we've kept going (even though unhappy underneath) until such time it would least disrupt everyone else and we can be free.

The strangest thing though, despite the glaring reality all around me, was that I sided with men and not with women in these situations until relatively recently. I thought a woman should get on with it. Stop fussing and being so weak. So what, if you earn more than your husband but he thinks he's superior to you or someone grabs your breasts at work, it's not the end of the world. I'm strong. I can deal with this and other women should too. By showing that you're weak, men will not respect us, plus, it will do unnecessary damage to other people, many of whom you love.

I spent three decades watching my husband grope other women when he was drunk, which was often, and to my utter shame I very rarely said this was not ok. I didn't say to him it was not ok at the time and I didn't say it was not ok the next day. I suppose I was a coward. I hate confrontation and my husband was much better at arguing than me, twisting words, cleverly constructing false meanings which would always leave me confused, frustrated and upset. I was made to feel that it was my fault and that I'd lost some sort of battle of wits. So you never got to work through the issues and how to address them. In these instances, the retorts would always be vicious and aggressive, with no prospect of him admitting, let alone apologising for what he'd done. It's like those things never actually happened. Eventually, there doesn't seem much point in arguing, so you leave the problem well alone and build a life around it. You bend yourself completely out of shape. Perhaps that's what bullies aim for.

Once I nearly lost my job at Barclays Bank where I was earning an annual salary of over £100,000 (and that was 20 years ago), because my husband sexually harassed my female boss at a company dinner, which by the way, I attended too. Note that nothing was ever said to him, but I was hauled up in front of HR and nearly lost my job because of his actions. I didn't tackle him about it. Just to add to my embarrassment she was the first appointed Head of Diversity at the bank.

I think that part of this is that I'm from (what was then described as) a working-class background that actually means I lack confidence and don't have an educated family network that would understand what having a career meant, or the relevance of sexist behaviour or even that it mattered. Anyhow, female members of my family had probably been through it too domestically, not that they ever said, and if they've put up with it, so should you.

But the transition from sexual harassment at home or

socially to sexual harassment in the workplace started to very, very slowly change my attitude. I think that it's the work situation and not the domestic or societal situation which has led us to the #metoo and #timesup 'campaign'. Workplace harassment whether sexual or otherwise just became less acceptable to me than social harassment. I'm not sure why but I think this is a very important point. Anyhow, although I've attempted to give a cultural and personal context to my eventual business success, I'm getting ahead of myself . . .

CHAPTER 5
The goldfish bowl

"I've learned that people will forget what you said, people will forget what you did, but people will never forget how you made them feel."

Maya Angelou

I found out a few months ago that the most popular women on dating websites are attractive, slim, young and educated but not too educated. The most popular men are wealthy and well-educated. Men want good looking young women. Women want wealthy intelligent men. Men overstate their height and women understate their weight. At all ages the average woman's ideal man is roughly the same age as her. So, as she gets older, she prefers someone the same age. No matter how old he is, the average man's ideal woman is 22. He could be 18, 40 or 75, he's still attracted to, and believes he can attract, a young woman. You may recall that I met my husband at 22 and he was 30.

Richard Gere with his somewhat younger wife

Richard Gere is over 70 years old. He recently married his 30-something Spanish girlfriend and has become a dad again. Caitlin Moran of *The Times* and *The Sunday Times* commented: **"As is the custom in our culture (men fall) for a woman 30 years younger ... because experiential parity and shared cultural reference points just aren't, at the end of the day, as much fun as some lovely perky tits."** Well, quite.

It helps that Richard Gere has $100 million to his name. Whichever way you cut it, both socially and professionally most men still have an over inflated view of their physical and professional talents despite the facts. They generally just feel they're much better looking and much smarter than they actually are. A famous Hewlett Packard internal report found that men apply for a job (or promotion) when they meet only 60 percent of the qualifications, but women apply only if they meet 100 percent. Ernesto Reuben, a professor at Columbia Business School, published a study in 2011, showing men consistently rated their performance on a set of maths problems to be 30 percent better than it was.

There's lots of other research to prove my point, especially in the workplace. Even though 37 percent of women working full time in the UK earn more than their husbands or partners, it's noticeable that when women go into a profession the overall salary levels drop, as if it can't actually be too difficult after all. Men ask for pay rises five times more often than women, they apply for jobs when they're under-qualified, they feel perfectly entitled to give you advice or contradict you even though you're eminently better qualified and more experienced. As Alexandra Petri put it: **"Too often I've seen a woman standing politely listening to a loud man's bad ideas about the field she has spent her life in."**

But what drives me mad is not that men often believe they are so much better than they really are and are keen to tell you so. It's that women tend to think the opposite of themselves and that really doesn't help.

Despite the fact that my husband was born in 1953 and grew up in the sexist culture of the 1960s and 1970s, he was a real advocate for women in the workplace. It's perverse that he was proud of my work achievements and genuinely wanted me to succeed professionally, as he did for our two daughters, and yet often he treated women badly. Maybe there was an inner conflict that he faced, battling between huge cultural and social pressure to act 'like a man' in the pub, at work and the rugby club, but being proud of my career and wanting me to go further. How that played out in his head, I don't know. I do think his attitude helped my professional confidence in one way and I owe him a lot for that.

Nevertheless, even if a woman is self-aware enough to estimate her true capability, there's still a 30 percent 'confidence gap' between what she views as her corporate worth compared to a man of the same skills and experience. It's not a level playing field and you can't get promoted (or listened to) on that basis. What dooms our corporate progress therefore is not our ability, but this discriminating and pervasive perception, and often our decision not to bother opposing it because it's stacked against us from the beginning. We also too often indulge such men in their supposed intellectual superiority, so it perpetuates and endorses their beliefs in this respect.

The societal and cultural backdrop that surrounded me and how it's formed my attitude to sexism is important as it's shaped my values and thinking. But my experience as shaped by my professional context is an essential element too. At this point I understood that you would get sexually harassed but I didn't yet know that people who shout loud, cheat and backstab their colleagues seem to float to the top. They crush kinder and nicer people both male and female, on the way through.

I eventually got a degree in graphic design. If you remember, I wasn't that great at academic exams, but I really was rather good at drawing. After qualifying I began work in London as a designer. By this time, it was 1984. This was a proper job and a career - well it was to me. Coming from a poor background with an under-educated family made me ambitious. I was keen to prove myself worthy in the world of work. It could be my ticket out of the working classes into the exalted status of the middle class. I was also curious, quick to grasp things and hard-working, so it seemed to me that it could be possible in a meritocratic society.

In my first post-graduate job as a designer, I worked for Howard in a pretty famous design studio in London. He was 6ft 4 and big in every sense of the word. Booming voice, extreme views, large fat stomach, big beard. He looked like a slightly dishevelled Father Christmas. He would get drunk most lunchtimes and stagger around the art studio where I worked, hungry after all that booze, devouring M&S sandwiches before examining our work. In those days there wasn't a computer at your desk you actually designed packaging, posters, brochures and adverts with pencils and pens, and on paper.

When Howard wasn't happy with what we produced he would shout and bawl at us. He was hugely intimidating and often said that my designs looked like they had been drawn with a DC. I didn't know what a DC was. No such thing as Google to look things up. When I eventually plucked up the courage to ask what that meant, he shouted at me yet again, and explained it meant a 'dog's cock'. That pretty much summed up the culture of the place.

We had a big boss over us called Judy somebody. She was middle aged, and her management style was to act like the worst type of man. She was stern and aggressive. Hard and cold. Prim and lacking humour or warmth. She definitely terrorised her way to the top. This was my first ever proper job. Howard was my first ever proper boss. I knew even then though, that a woman trying to 'out man' a man on the aggression front was a perilous tactic because you're just not as naturally assertive or lacking in empathy. You don't have the tools.

At one meeting in front of a good handful of managers, Howard, reasonably drunk after lunch, was disagreeing loudly and dismissively with Judy even though she was his boss and her points were well made. He just leant forward right into her face and loudly declared in front of everyone that her problem was that she needed a good fuck. Everyone knew she was married, not single. Even so the inference of course was that he was the man for the job, even though he made it clear he found her physically unattractive. Somehow, he would do her a sexual favour because clearly this would be the best sex of her life and her difficulties and anxieties as a female boss would fall away.

I was shocked, but I thought she deserved it. Professionally, you can't act like a man if you're a woman, any fool can see that won't work. I guess I was on his side even though he was a total arsehole, because I didn't respect her management style and thought she made the plight of working women worse.

I had numerous other bosses who were arseholes too. They've groped me, asked to sleep with me or cornered me on business trips. One who was married and whose wife had just had a baby girl, knocked on my hotel door when I was 18; I was working as an office temp in the summer holidays and I was asked to go abroad for a couple of days to reconcile some accounts with our French counterparts. That night he banged on my hotel door asking if he could sleep with me and why else did I think he had brought me on this business trip? I felt pretty naïve. I had never had sex with anyone before. I was culpable for going on the trip and not realising. My fault. He was seriously affronted when I said no and obviously, I lost that job too.

Although there are lots more examples, two further instances stick in my mind that fail to dim with time. We had moved to the north west of England with my husband's job in 1991, and the first serious incident was when I was as a senior lecturer at Staffordshire University Business School. I was also studying for my MBA in the evenings and the whole cohort, about 30 of us went on an exchange trip to the Grand Canyon University in Arizona. The course leader was Mike Carrick and he was middle aged and white.

His name is etched on my memory because you never forget the name of people who abuse you. He was well known for harassing female students. It was the culture of the business school there and you were expected to handle it. One student who was in her 30s was so relentlessly hassled on the trip, not by him but by one of his colleagues, she moved hotels at her own expense just to escape. She could barely afford it but she felt she was in real danger.

During the exchange trip I woke up in my hotel bedroom in the middle of the night and the old, fat, grey Carrick was standing at the end of the bed wanting to have sex. He had obviously got a key somehow and let himself in. I think he was drunk. In the dark I managed with a huge amount of difficulty to talk him out of raping me and he left. I was married with a toddler and a baby at home.

He got found out by some of the other students and rather unusually, a complaint was made against him, not by me. When we got back, I was asked by the Dean of Faculty to make a formal grievance so that the university could attempt to make a case against him, although it was by no means clear if he would be sacked. As a shameful coward, I declined, even under a lot of pressure from my Dean and others. Why? Because my life would have been an utter misery and I'm convinced eventually I would be the one who had to leave. I was worried that this would follow me around into other job interviews and I would literally be unemployable. We desperately needed the money at the time. I was years from landing my well-paid job at Barclays Bank.

I didn't tell my husband about any of this. If I had, as a working-class man with a police record when younger, brought up in a council house in Preston, he would have gone around to beat him up or worse. That would definitely mess my kids up, and yes, I would lose my job again, so anyway I looked at it, it didn't feel worth it. Selfish I know.

The second instance was my next role after being an academic. I knew I wasn't going to progress far at the university even though now I was armed with an MBA. By this time the children were school age so I thought I could manage a less flexible full-time job. I had a handful of interviews for a variety of organisations and at two of these I was asked what my childcare arrangements were. This really annoyed me. I guessed they didn't ask male candidates the same question. Again, I didn't complain because I couldn't see how making a complaint at an interview before you heard whether you'd got the job would make any difference. Rather it was likely to preclude you from an offer.

Eventually, I landed a job in the private sector as a marketing and sales director in a factory in Manchester. There were around 100 or so employees and the whole management team was middle-aged, white and male as was the norm. It was quite clear to me that I was a token female appointment, but I didn't care. I knew I could do the job and I got a good salary and a company car. To give myself the best chance of getting this role and to avoid the 'what are your childcare arrangements' question, I didn't ever mention that I was married or a mother. Not to anyone, either at the interview or during my whole time as an employee. No photographs of the children on my desk for me.

During my first week I met all the other male senior managers that made up the management team, except one, the Production Manager. When I met him at last, he introduced himself and said that he was going to give me a Manchester welcome. Much was made that Londoners (like me) were cold and aloof, but northerners were warm and chatty. He then pinned me up against the wall and stuck his tongue hard down my throat in front of the MD and some of the other management team. Everyone laughed, and this was seen as a jolly friendly and welcoming thing to do. Nobody missed a heartbeat, no one wondered how that might have felt for me. If you want to know by the way, I felt totally violated and humiliated and wanted to throw up.

But of course, I said nothing. As Nicola Sturgeon said, who would I have said it to? They owned and ran the company where systematic male domination, terrorising staff, rules of hierarchy and intolerance of anyone that didn't fit, was the workplace culture. I did nothing. What could I have done? What action would have been taken and by who? They had a form of self-regulation so where would that put me professionally? Did I tell my husband? Of course not.

Why was the business world like this? I couldn't find answers anywhere, not even in religious teachings. The world's biggest encyclopaedia (the internet) was not yet fully formed. I had no mentors or family support, so I spent a lot of time trying to work out how to navigate corporate life in order to succeed. Or perhaps I should just give up? But I didn't want to give in and drop out of it altogether like so many women. I wanted to earn a better life for me and my children. Instead, I worked out a way to navigate this standard state of affairs. I was determined to prove that a woman, one from a deprived background and someone who didn't believe in lying, shouting and belittling, could make a success of themselves somehow ….

It seemed to me that men sexually harassed or abused you because it was ok. The masculine norm. I don't think I'm blaming them actually. It was just the environment in which you lived. It felt that, at no time, did a man have any thought at all as to how it would make you feel. It's all about the culture, system, environment they'd created – because they built it and it's all around them, they can't see or feel it. You're soaked in the masculine norm. So, although I think there are a lot of very good men and most will hate the gorilla alpha males that bully their way to the top as much as I do . . . they don't notice that the patriarchy is in charge. They don't see the bias nature of the structures around them and therefore they have inequality blindness. That's why they don't think there's a problem.

It's their rules and their world and they're richer, bigger and stronger. If you think about it, if you're a middle-aged privileged white man, then you grew up in it. You inherited the rules, the language, the culture, the macro-environment, the carrots and the sticks, so of course you can't see it from another perspective. It's like being a goldfish. You've been swimming around in water your whole life you can't imagine any other environment. How could you conceive what it might feel like for someone else to be swimming in water if they haven't been in it before? It's almost impossible.

As a woman, particularly in a work environment where a man had greater power and influence, you would be sexually assaulted or abused because it was fine for him to help himself to whatever he wanted. The trying wasn't wrong. You wouldn't be punished for trying, rather you would be applauded. That was the culture - you're allowed to try. Whether he got what he wanted was up to you, so trying, groping, sticking your tongue down your throat is ok. It was absolutely ok. If you complained about the trying, women and men would instantly turn on you. Get on with it. If you don't want it, say so somehow but don't embarrass the man, don't make him feel rejected or belittled, that upsets the way everything works, and anyhow he will have his revenge.

The spectre of ground-breaking women such as Dr Frances Hogan* was hanging over me. I only had historical figures to inspire me. There were no female role models in truly influential public and private sector roles and the power of social media was still a way off.

Hogan was an unmarried mother and given the immense discrimination she faced during her whole career you would think she was intimidating and formidable. But she believed that being strident held you back and is famous for saying: **"Don't shout about it, don't make a fuss. Just get it done."** Then there was the ethos of Harry S Truman: **"It's amazing what you can accomplish if you do not care who gets the credit."** These attitudes, which made so much sense to me, was my mantra of how I was supposed to act and react. It seemed very dignified. My path has been repeatedly blocked, obstructed and diverted but I was supposed to quietly go around these inconveniences and not noisily through them. Crack on. But if you believe that, which I did, how do you get to the top in the first place? Surely, you're invisible if you don't take the credit and shy away from plaudits?

I began to work out that society deemed that a man trying to abuse you in some way was not wrong - the way you deal with it, was right or wrong. As I read somewhere about the 1970s, the convention of the time was 'women resisted but men insisted'. Dealing with it, was what defined society's judgement of you as a woman, not the act that put you in that position. This is what I managed to work out. You could attempt to out-bully a man who was doing that. Shout them down, kick and scream, but it wasn't in my nature and I wasn't convinced that in those days it would've worked.

In order to navigate this backdrop of sexual harassment, it seemed to me that I had three reactionary options. 1) If you go with it and sleep with the guy you would run the risk of being perceived as a slut or a man stealer. Both male and female opinion. 2) If you said "no" aggressively you would be a feminist bitch. Male and female opinion. I thought, then and perhaps other people did too, that feminist was a derogatory term. Added to that, the reason why you said no would, from a man's point of view, be because you were frigid or lesbian.

I thought that was what a feminist was; a frigid or lesbian woman. I'm not a lesbian. I desire men but love my women friends. In fact, I would quite like to be a lesbian because I think you would probably do less washing and tidying up, but then nobody admitted to knowing a lesbian, let alone being one.

So, the two polarised options were being branded a slut or lesbian, or 3) you found a humorous-polite way of getting out of it. If you could master that art, you would be praised and prized by both sexes; an elegant operator that would emerge relatively unscathed whilst flattering the tryer. It was the best possible solution. Well, it was for male-dominated workplace harmony because his behaviours weren't his responsibility, it was your responsibility to deal with it.

I was not from a well-educated family and I was not born middle class with the confidence that often bestows, nor was I naturally assertive. There are so many people in this position who don't have a voice. This reasoning in my head, made me feel I couldn't turn to anyone. An outsider again, even if increasingly this wasn't true. Who would I talk to? My mum? My dad? My husband? My boss? My female work colleagues? I didn't come from a background where you had those types of conversations.

I could go on and on and on with hundreds more examples and so could thousands of other women like me, of my age and younger. Then, you just thought it was a thing that happened, and you had to find a way to navigate it, otherwise it would ruin your career or your marriage or both, and worse it might affect your children. I would guess the majority of women who have tweeted #metoo have been through this and they just want to let you know they have. They're not making any capital out of it. It's just that after silently putting up with all that crap, they want to let someone, anyone, know how they've repeatedly felt in the past.

CHAPTER 6
Belly flop

"When a man is successful, he is liked by both men and women. When a woman is successful, people of both genders like her less."

Sheryl Sandberg

Growing up I never knew anyone in a position of corporate authority who was a woman and definitely not a mother, either in real life, films, tv programmes or books. I'd seen female head teachers, women overseeing typists and matrons in charge of nurses (think Hattie Jacques in *Carry On Doctor*) but that was it. Everyone had mums who either stayed at home or who had part time jobs as cleaners, shop assistants, factory girls and lowly office workers. But post-marriage they never entered into the world of full-time work, neither had they been college- or university- educated so they might compete and get promoted.

At my all girls' grammar school there were lots of wealthy (in my eyes) students who would obviously go to university and initially go into 'the professions', but I never remember seeing any of their mothers. I can't say whether they were career people, as I never met them and didn't mix in that circle anyway. Even so, across the whole class spectrum at school, there was still a strong attitude that educating young women was a bit of a waste of time, because they would have children and then give up work, so what was the point.

That was in the 1970s and I am not sure that attitude has been eradicated even now. For example, The Tokyo Medical School apologised after confirming they altered entrance exam scores from 2006 through to 2018, to ensure more men became doctors than women. As *The Boston Globe* reported:

"The investigation found that in this year's (2018) entrance exams the school reduced all applicants' first-stage test scores by 20 percent and then added at least 20 points for male applicants . . . It said similar manipulations had occurred for years because the school wanted fewer female doctors

since it anticipated they would shorten or halt their careers after becoming mothers."

But despite the attitude back then and apparently still now, I did get a glimpse of two unusual role models in my late teens who were not only in corporate authority but were mums too. Neither had been educated beyond secondary school.

Before I started my graphic design degree, I went to work in a ten-storey office block doing relatively boring admin work and that's where I met my husband. These were the days when women worked in a typing pool to type up the letters and memos handwritten by men, and the telex room was cutting edge technology. Your desk had papers, pens, in-trays and out-trays. Mobile phones and computers as we know them now, had not been invented.

Maureen Keppler worked in that office and she was a mum and one of the bosses! This was a real revelation to me. She was magnificent. Funny and sassy and bloody good at her job, and she also looked amazing in her ladylike but professional work outfits and it dawned on me that she had a work compatible femininity. She oozed seniority but not arrogance. She gave male contemporaries a hard time if they stepped out of line but they sort of admired her for it and yet she was still undoubtedly a woman. No one would describe her as a lesbian or frigid. I can only imagine now, what grief she put up with, but her husband worked there too and maybe that helped.

The second role model was my aunt Anne, who was also my godmother. I went to stay with her for the weekend one time and had to go to her workplace to be picked up. I'd never been before. I had 15 aunts and uncles that were alive at that time, but she was a managing director in a small company that had something to do with the airline industry. When I sat in the reception area she emerged, again in a tailored work suit and I realised that although she may be the mother of my cousin, she had another life that was separate. It was a revelation and I was stunned. This was a woman who was one of eight very poor children who began her childhood sleeping in one bed with her three sisters.

She had an assumed but modest air of authority and was clearly respected for what she knew and not for being a woman, a mother or wife. There might not be any fictional role models for me to aspire to, but there were two women in real life that gave me a tiny glimpse of what might just be possible. I wanted to be like Maureen and Anne.

I got my degree. It was in a non-academic subject but what the hell and I started to work as a designer in London albeit under the famous Howard and Judy. Then of course I got married and was soon pregnant which was what you were expected to do. I didn't predict what it was like to be pregnant and working. I hadn't imagined that my sense of smell would become so acute that I could tell what each person in the office had for breakfast just by walking past them on my way to throw up in the toilet for the second time that morning. But if you were serious about your career, you didn't let on and did those things silently without leaving any clues that it might possibly affect your work performance. I didn't want to give anyone a reason to demote or side line me because I was going to be a new mum.

My pragmatic approach to pregnancy was wasted though because my career stalled. Well actually it stopped completely. I could no longer commute to London and work long hours in the advertising industry with two young children. The thought that my husband might take on some childcare responsibility was out of the question. He was eight years older than me and at that time was earning at least double my salary so economically that didn't make sense and it was never discussed anyhow.

I wanted to continue working in some capacity and not give up altogether. I wanted to stay in the game because I was worried that if I had a break, I might never get on the ladder again. So, I decided that becoming a lecturer might be a good idea. Yes, I wasn't very academic, but I do have great communication skills (see, I'm getting better at promoting myself) so I thought teaching adults about design and business could play to my abilities.

I wrote to every tertiary education establishment within a 30-mile radius, often not getting a reply but eventually worked part-time at an art college then later I got a job at a university (as I've described the lovely Business School at Staffordshire University). It was a smart move; although full-time, I could have gratuitous amounts of holiday and get home early if I didn't have to see students. This job was unusual then because by its nature it was flexible. I read, researched, assessed dissertations and prepared lectures at home, after I'd cooked the dinner and the kids were in bed.

Nevertheless, my mother-in-law saw this move towards full time work as a huge threat to the family and she was convinced this would have a detrimental effect on our children. They would become drug addicts or hard drinkers, or at the very least be rude and unruly. The irony was lost on her that her own son had been in trouble with the police in his youth and was a practicing alcoholic, even though she exercised an almost constant home presence before and after school.

In her mind I would be absent, and they would get into trouble in the vacuum that would create. It would of course be harmful to my husband; how would the washing, ironing and cooking get done? My own mum, though largely silent on the subject, periodically uttered barbed comments every time the children were naughty or had a blip at school. They were victim to my selfish wish to pursue a career.

In defence of my husband, he was fine with cooking and washing as part of this deal and did so without me ever having to ask. This was unusual among his generation, as demonstrated by Sir Tony Blair who was born in the same year (1953). Our former Prime Minster revealed he hasn't done housework, laundry, a weekly grocery shop or cooked a family meal since the month he entered Number 10 in 1997. His wife, although unfairly maligned in the UK press for some reason I don't understand, is a barrister and Queen's Counsel specialising in employment, discrimination and public law. She's a mother of three with a demanding job, so it's not as if she's knocking about the house with nothing to do but look after Tony's laundry and cook his meals. In comparison, my husband might have appeared saintly in this respect, but cleaning the toilet eluded him for some three decades.

Interestingly my mother-in-law was a school dinner lady and my mum worked part time as an office clerk. You were 'allowed' to do this as a woman if it was secondary to the family and in no way involved ambition or career advancement. It was perceived as very bad to do this as a woman if you had ideas that might involve professional aspirations because it was selfish, and the family would lose out. I was therefore very careful not to outwardly dominate in family situations. When I went back into industry initially, I played down my role as a mother when at work. As my career progressed again, I pointedly avoided revealing I had children at all, so it couldn't be used against me. It was also clear that outwardly successful women were not liked much, either socially or professionally, so I made sure I was modest and didn't talk about my achievements.

Sheryl Sandberg, the Chief Operating Officer of Meta (previously Facebook) has written about the challenge this presents for women. Her conclusion is that when a man is successful, he's well liked. When a woman does well, people like her less. Most of us want to be liked. But if our success means that others don't like us, especially our female family and friends, how motivated are we to do well? Bullies don't mind being disliked, I guess it's a badge of honour and they can misinterpret it as respect. Sandberg admits that she's undermined her own accomplishments for fear that others would be turned off. I think I've done that too because I wanted to be respected and liked.

The interface between my home and work life involved immense planning and was run like a machine to make sure everyone was happy. It was utterly exhausting, compounded by the fact that while still working at the university I started studying for an MBA at night because I felt I wasn't being taken seriously. I had yet to realise it was sexual and not academic discrimination that was the cause. I also felt I had to simultaneously succeed professionally and as a mother, otherwise I couldn't socially justify why I went to work. To make it more pressured my husband was frequently abroad, although what he got up to when he was there, I didn't want to think about.

I love being a mother. It's the most monumental thing I've ever done in my life and always will be. I'm so proud of my two daughters and how they've turned out that sometimes I could burst, and naturally my husband should take a lot of credit for that too. I don't know why society dictated that I had to be saddled with crippling worries about 'selfishness' in having a career for the 20 years when they were at home. It's wrong really that professionally I've had to suppress my maternal side or hide the fact that I was a mother at all, in order to minimise work discrimination. You get a hard enough time if you're a female, but a female with children is even worse.

Anyhow, at Barclays Bank and in my following jobs, my design background had morphed into more general marketing and communication roles. I rejected being a marketer that promoted consumer products, because getting teenagers to eat pot noodles or old age pensioners to buy Stannah chair lifts didn't feel intellectually stimulating enough for me. Also, frankly, it's too easy. Instead, I became more and more involved in 'social marketing' or behavioural economics as it's sometimes known. How do you influence people's behaviour? Not buying behaviour but their social behaviour for a good moral reason, rather than just selling stuff? Now that's interesting.

At Barclays my role was to change internal behaviours across a base of thousands of employees in relation to software development, training and management. It was incredibly technical which I won't bore you with, but I was fascinated. From there I took what I learned and left this very, very well-paid job and moved to an environmental charity. My husband literally cried when I resigned as I reduced my wages by two thirds, but it's probably the best thing I've ever done in my career. I felt so fulfilled.

I had a marketing and programme department with a research team, event managers, print production unit, programme co-ordinators, campaign managers and press office of some 75 or so people. It was still difficult juggling parental responsibilities, but the children were older now and it was definitely a bit easier. The department was somewhat directionless and not very efficient to start with, but it had some great people with huge potential. With all that natural talent if I could get the culture right, I thought something very special could happen.

The charity had a government grant to deliver national campaigns and environmental programmes to combat, what we called, 'local environmental quality' problems. These issues cost local authorities money and resources which were desperately needed elsewhere. Things such as graffiti, litter, flyposting, abandoned vehicles, flytipping, dog fouling, low level anti-social behaviour, neighbourhood noise, avoidable household waste and so on are an unnecessary drain on resources. If we could get the public to change their behaviours then more council money could be allocated to health, homelessness, parks, libraries, social care and education. We agreed annual marketing and communication plans aligned to government priorities with the relevant minister, including key performance indicators that would prove our positive impact across the UK. Broadly we worked to help improve the local environment for residents, trying to reduce unnecessary council spending and regenerate run-down communities.

Our staff were amazing. I knew they could be great. I implemented flexible working (this was over 20 years ago) which was a bit tricky to get past the board, but I managed it. We had a nine-day fortnight across the team, which meant a slightly increased working day but essentially everyone got a day off every other week on top of their holiday allowance. You can't have each member of staff disappear every Friday, that won't work, especially in a press office. So, they had to invent and manage a fair system for rotating days off between them, which they did.

I monitored it in a number of ways, and it showed conclusively that we had less sick days, better employee retention, increased efficiency, improved customer satisfaction and staff were generally happier. Put simply, hands down it made both business and economic sense. I became a huge advocate for flexible working policies from then on.

Within a short time, our team became one of the country's leading experts on social marketing. We got the whole country to clear up after their dogs, reduce neighbourhood noise, litter, flytipping and graffiti, decrease the number of abandoned vehicles and increase their recycling rates among many other issues. We taught council's how to deal with these behaviours and how to design them out of, or design them into, the local street environment so their communities felt safer and less polarised.

As this is partly a business book, I think I should explain what I learnt and how we managed to get real results in changing, or influencing, public behaviour. It can also be used to influence buying behaviour and customer preference for your product or service too of course . . .

Marketing is everything. Everything. It's a philosophy and not a process. It includes marketing, business development, communication, brand and sales. It's about putting the end recipient or customer at the centre of every single business decision you make including all elements of your marketing strategy. It's about winning people around to your values or philosophy and then keeping them there, so they become active advocates and ambassadors. When you've nailed it, every one of your staff and every touch point will be orientated around the reason why you're in business in the first place. Each person whether they're the cleaner or the financial director will be trained to understand why this matters. It must come through in your customer communications, your payment systems, your delivery choices, your branding, the language you use, the images you project, the media channels you select etc . . . all set up for the benefit of the customer or the groups you're targeting and not the company.

In order to do that you need to know everything about your target end user or customer. Create a profile of them so you can visualise them. This makes it easier for your staff to understand who they're dealing with. Decide typically how old they might be, where they go on holiday, what car they drive, what their house or flat looks like, how much they earn, their values, what media they regularly use. Work out what their favourite film or book might be, their music preferences and importantly the language, type of vocabulary and tone of voice they prefer. Then find out how they research, buy and use the product or service they get from your competitors. How does your archetypal customer gather the knowledge that enables them to make the decision to buy? What prompts that decision? What puts them off? What is it that would make them choose to use you and not someone else? Think it through, don't just hope they'll buy from you, that's way too scary.

In terms of social marketing, it's the same process. If you want to get dog owners to use waste bins, what's stopping them? What's going on inside their head when that just leave their dogs faeces in a park for someone to step in and, unaware, drag through the carpet in their home? What types of messages will they respond to? Are their cultural or religious barriers? You can't even begin to construct a public campaign if you don't understand the barriers to doing the right thing. If you haven't done this type of research you're just guessing and wasting time and money. You're making huge assumptions and it's literally pointless.

To attract and retain customers (or target the public) you must lower or mitigate the barriers whether perceived or real, that put them off. Yes, you do need to big up the b enefits of a purchase or a course of action, but too often businesses just focus on benefits and forget about removing barriers. If the barrier is price, what can you put in place that will overcome that hurdle? If they're put off by the length of time between ordering and receiving the product, how can you get it to them quicker? If you're trying to stop flytipping, why is someone not using a waste site?

From a corporate business point of view, gather all this intelligence and only then should you design your business from the customer backwards and not from your service or product forwards. Use this information to construct organisation processes that are convenient for them and not you. Use the language on your website, in your social media posts and in personal interactions that make them feel comfortable and definitely scrap any use of jargon which has the effect of excluding and belittling. It's just intellectual wanking. As I used to say to our staff: **"If our clients don't understand what we're saying, it's because we're failing to explain it simply enough and that's our fault not theirs."**

Use the marketing channels they already use, not what you like. I remember some of our board members saying we should be on *Radio 4* more. My reply to that is always the same, although I put it somewhat more politely at the time, but the gist is: **"You might listen to *Radio 4,* but our customers like Instagram, so why would I do that?"**

Go further. Recruit staff that mirror your target audience or at the very least have a natural affinity with them. Design your visual brand to reflect them too. Again, the answer to a director colleague who said to me that they didn't like our company logo was: **"We've researched it to death and it really chimes with our target audience. They love it and it's for them not for you, so if you don't like it that's a really good sign, thank you so much for vindicating the design."** Then go even further still. Are the backdrops on your zoom calls and the templates on your email signatures appropriate for your customers? If they come to your office do the pictures you hang in reception, the soap in your toilets, the coffee cups, fit with them? Absolutely think through every detail. This is what brand is, the sum total and coherence of all those things.

Too often I've seen 'push' marketing, where a company just tells anyone that will listen how great they are with no thought of the audience. A better description could be 'pushy' marketing because it's not about listening but shouting. Master the art of 'pull' marketing where you listen and understand and draw your clients into an engaging mutual relationship that lasts. In essence as I've said, marketing is a philosophy. If you're the boss you're the person in the organisation who should relentlessly champion, safeguard and represent the views and the experience of customers, ensuring all business decisions and processes are made for their convenience.

I continue to use this as the operating basis for all my work and voluntary roles because the subject matter or sector doesn't matter, the methodology is the same. I often get asked why I've had such a varied marketing career and how I've managed to move between the public, charity and private sectors in a vast range of areas from financial services and health to technical research and food, to education and local environment. Or as one of my mates put it - from dog shit to tax returns. Well, I don't see it like that. To me the roles have always been the same – put the target customer at the centre of every decision you make, recruit great people and develop a positive culture so they can thrive. Then create a totally immersive brand and messaging that will get you noticed by the people who want to be part of it because they share your values.

Using this as my guide our charity started to get noticed and we began to feature all over the national media and trade press. It was a key aim to get our work highlighted in the media or use well known people to promote or sponsor our campaigns. I spoke at conferences, lobbied government bodies and appeared on radio or tv on an almost weekly basis to get our message across. I was once dubbed: **"The unthinking man's Carol Vorderman."** To this day I don't know if that's a compliment or not. My kids just thought it was amusing that I was on the radio and telly an awful lot, as did my friends.

When you deal with the media as much as we did, you get to know the researchers on news programmes and the journalists on national and regional newspapers, and mostly you develop pretty good relationships with them. Once you get in their book of contacts, they'll ring or email you every time something in your sector comes up. I've been interviewed literally hundreds and hundreds of times by most of the UK's tabloids and broadsheets and radio stations such as *Radio 5 Live, The Asian Network, Radio 2, Talk-*

Sport, *Radio 4* and so on. I also spent a good deal of my time being interviewed on tv programmes such as *CNN International*, *Sky News*, *ITV News*, *Channel 4 News*, B*BC Breakfast*, *The Today Programme*, *The Politics Show* and *The Culture Show*, by the likes of Tony Wilson, Edwina Curry, John Humphreys, Jon Snow, Kirsty Young etc etc.

We also had to work with 'celebrities', which I hate with a passion. That involved the frustrating experience of dealing with their agents to back our charitable campaigns or sponsorship events. The worst celebrities I've come across are the three self-important and rude Atomic Kitten 'singers', the chef Keith Floyd (who I loved but was a real handful), Ann Widdecombe (who never listens or lets you get a word in edgeways), Antony Worrall Thompson (incredibly rude to my staff which is unforgiveable) and Max Clifford (who turned up drunk to an event we organised, and not for the first time), no one knew he was a paedophile then. The nicest being Ruby Wax (extremely professional and very well briefed), Jill Dando (a delight in every way but sadly no longer with us), Sir Trevor McDonald (what a truly lovely man), Mary Berry (quite rightly now the UK's de facto grandma), Veer Bhadra Mishra (*TIME* magazine's 'Hero of the Planet' famed for cleaning up The Ganges) and Ricky Tomlinson (cannot do enough to help with your cause).

However, despite this background and vast experience in dealing with the industry around it, I made a single catastrophic error.

The media love a long running theme where they can show further incidences that back up their theory. Boris Johnson, who you may have heard of, was at the time, MP for Henley and editor of *The Spectator*. He had accused Liverpudlians of **"mawkish sentimentality"**. This was after the death of hostage Kenneth Bigley by Muslim militants who released a video of him being beheaded. Boris declared that theirs was **"a society that has become hooked on grief and likes to wallow in a sense of vicarious victimhood"** stretching back to the Hillsborough disaster where 97 adults and children died. He didn't say this as an aside, it was in an article in his magazine. The media picked up on it immediately and there were a couple of days analysing his career and his past gaffes (little did they know how many more there were to come), with calls for him to be sacked (nothing changes).

On 16 October 2004 he was forced to apologise by the then Tory leader Michael Howard and made to travel up to the north west. More in-depth stories ensued on his trip to meet and apologise to local people for insulting them. The theme is that London people have no idea about living up north and that the 'north – south divide', or rather 'the capital versus the rest of the country divide', is alive and well.

As is normal, journalists then scout around to see if there is anything else that will chime with the theme. Our press office suddenly got inundated. It had been reported that I'd spoken at a conference in London and said in my opening gambit: **"I would like to start by saying that Wigan is the arse end of the world."** I then remembered the occasion. The conference was on the regeneration of deprived communities, where I was last to speak on stage. I'd been invited as I'd written a book about the 'broken windows' theory and how it encouraged inner city crime.

The theory was first described by Wilson & Kelling in 1982. Basically, they argued that if a window is broken and left unrepaired, residents and visitors will conclude that no one cares and no one is in charge. Inevitably more windows will be broken, and the sense of lawlessness will spread from that building onto the street, sending a community message that anything goes. I argued in my book therefore that relatively minor problems like litter, graffiti, flyposting, abandoned vehicles and flytipping **"are all the equivalent of broken windows. That is to say, an invitation to more serious crimes . . . This is an epidemic theory of anti-social behaviour: something that is catching and contagious. It can start with a broken window and spread to an entire community."**

My message to the audience of local authority employees, cleaning contractors and town planners was simple and economically efficient in the long run. If you can design out these problems or keep tight control of cleanliness and the appearance of community spaces, it would have a dramatic effect on crime levels but more importantly would make them safer places for residents.

It was hosted by Nick Ross, which was entirely relevant because at the time he was presenting the popular BBC programme *Crimewatch*. This word-for-word reference to Wigan was factually correct but it was weeks ago. The journos could not believe their luck. They could keep on with the 'Londoners think they're better than northerners' tack, bring up the Boris story again, and even better, legitimately use the word "arse" in their headlines. It was a gold-plated gift.

The initial report was in fact a tiny two-line throwaway comment in a small magazine called *Regeneration and Renewal*. I knew these guys and they had been at the conference and heard the speech. They understood I was trying to explain to that rather privileged London audience (the place where I was born), that not all deprivation is found in inner city

London boroughs. I should know because I live way outside London. All day the conference had given examples that just weren't relevant in the north west where I lived and where my children were brought up. As I was last to speak I wanted to point this out, albeit in a humorous way, because it was so typical and it made me angry.

As *Regeneration and Renewal* reported in a follow-up piece: **"We believe that Sue's comments, though misjudged, were made in a light-hearted spirit and that's how we treated them."** And that's what they did, they reported the context and that it was ironic but stated word-for-word my hugely misjudged quote about Wigan. The conference was a couple of weeks beforehand, but the national media picked up those two lines because it fitted with the article by Boris. With my media experience, as soon as I remembered it, I knew it would explode. A massive shit show ensued. Yes, massive.

"Wigan Rear!" howled *The Sun* and the *Daily Mirror* (nice pun on Wigan Pier there) and lots of other headlines in every single daily national newspaper such as **"Wigan? It's the arse end of the world!** (Daily Mail). They were all calling for my head. **"George Orwell thought Wigan the epitome, the exemplar and the quintessence of 1930s urban industrial Britain"** wrote *The Times*: **Seventy years on Sue Nelson regards the Lancashire town as the arse end of the world."** I was mortified. My boss exacerbated the situation by immediately banning me from speaking to any journalist, thereby not allowing me to apologise profusely or give more detail. This is a real rookie error as anyone in PR or the media knows because there are unwritten rules for crisis management:

1. You have to seize the initiative away from journalists even

during a terrible crisis. Concentrate on <u>what</u> has happened, never why or how at the beginning. You have to explain exactly what happened, so they know the absolute facts of the situation and then, what you're doing about it. You must be seen to be doing the right thing.

2. Always show care and concern about the people involved (never what it cost or how it has affected you). Then show how you've got control of the situation and your commitment to putting it right or dealing with it.

3. Be absolutely truthful and relevant to the audience and never be aggressive.

The media have a huge expectation that they will be fed with information from the hand of the organisation or the person at the centre of the problem or event. If they don't get that, they will talk to just about anyone who can give them an opinion (they're called 'telly tarts' in the media). That allows personal feelings, anger, rumour and gossip to be at the centre. If that happens, your chances of being reported fairly or factually go out the window, because you cannot counter personal affrontery or deny if someone is angry. The media can go all out for subjective opinions from anyone willing to step in front of a microphone. If you speak to reporters quickly, they will still seek out telly tarts, but will do so from the perspective of verifying what you've said in the first instance.

I was contacted by a slew of journalists that I knew, but I had to tell them all that I was not allowed to comment. They couldn't believe it, as it was unusual to say the least. I begged my boss to reconsider but to no avail. BBC One's *North West Tonight* went on the hunt for telly tarts as I knew they would. They trooped off to the streets of Wigan to interview shoppers to ask if they were proud of their town or whether it was actually the arse end, as I had described it. Obvious what the answers to that was going to be. It began spiralling out of control and started being described as **"arsegate."** Oh dear God!

The *Manchester Evening News*, where I knew the editor fairly well, ran the front page headline: **"How dare she."** They thoughtfully added a telephone/text poll for their readers asking whether I should be sacked or not. Thankfully, 'not' was the eventual outcome, with 55% saying I should not be sacked.

The Wigan Evening Post who had never been gifted such a wonderful opportunity for their town to be the centre of national news, wasted no time in displaying the large headline on its front page: **"Fury as wigan branded arse-end of the world."** It was followed by pages and pages of quotes from local people about their indignation over the **"arsegate label"** and anger alongside opinions from Wigan's diaspora. Residents started turning up at our offices to shout abuse. Journalists tried to find out where I lived to doorstep me (only one managed it, *The Daily Mirror*) and my children got bullied at school. A few days later I got suspended from my job, mostly for my own protection.

Aside from the top line quote, and the statements that I was **"unavailable for comment"** and **"refused to comment"**, most of the reports were utter rubbish. Nobody had actually been to the conference except for the guys at *Regeneration and Renewal*, but many journalists wrote as if they had. They all mentioned that I was from London, but not that I was resident in the north west for well over a decade, as *The Times* put it: **"Ms Nelson is from London and does not live in the town she has**

vilified," forgetting to mention that I worked there and lived a few miles down the road. Or that I was on a couple of government bodies trying to get more investment and recognition for the area.

It was a shallow caricature stripped of context or any depth. One Swedish newspaper said that I had led a national campaign for cleaner streets and could hardly believe my eyes when I saw how filthy it was in the small town. All lies.

What was correct is that I made an incredibly stupid mistake. It was one for which I apologised many, many times later, writing letters to the local newspapers, to the local MP and to other affected parties because I had really harmed the image of the town. By then it was way too late. Apologies must be immediate, or they look suspicious.

My stupid comment was unintentional but that didn't matter, the damage was done. So many people had grafted to bring Wigan's image up above its abandoned industrial roots and I had just made it worse. Fuelled by anger at the injustice of swathes of people without a voice, the slip of my tongue had spectacularly backfired, and I should have known it. I don't regret many things in my life, but that ill-disciplined off-the-cuff comment is one of them.

I managed to hold on to my job after a disciplinary hearing, but I left soon after. I obviously couldn't carry on representing the organisation in the media any longer. Not that I wanted to. I'm very proud of the five years that I spent at that charity as we genuinely achieved extraordinary things there. But I felt the whiff of my big mistake would probably always follow me around and, I guess this can be seen as funny (just) all these years later, but I didn't want to only ever be known as **"the arse lady."** I promised myself that for the rest of my working life, I would still rail against unfairness and injustice whenever I could, just with much more care and not in front of large audiences or in the media.

CHAPTER 7
Swimming against the tide

We have one woman already on the board, so we are all done – it's someone else's turn."

Anonymous board member

I initially struggled to get another job because of my career hiccup. In the era of social media you can't hide such a thing. But I was still determined not to give up on my vocation and eventually I got on the job ladder again and rose higher and gradually earned more and more. I got other director positions using my social marketing experience to influence behaviours as before.

My favourite stint was in the health sector gaining real improvements in the reduction of death rates from a variety of cancers and other serious diseases. We achieved positive movement on getting people to present symptoms to their GP earlier. This obviously increases the chances of survival. It was immensely rewarding. I served on government bodies and worked as a non-executive in a range of charities. But although the actual day job was important to me and usually intellectually challenging, the work environment so often involved ridiculous office politics or overcoming entrenched personal interests that weren't at all relevant to the end user. So often I wanted to scream: **"Can we remember why we're here and doing this please? It's not about you and your petty personal agenda."**

Then by 2015, I just couldn't continue with the bruising battles at boardroom level or using so much unnecessary energy making a case for our customers or target markets. The posturing, bullying, lying and the perplexing disdain for employees and continued gender differential in pay just got too galling, as did the fight to get my voice heard as a woman around a boardroom table. I'd read and heard that equality and a more respectful workplace environment had dawned, but I couldn't find it in my paid or voluntary director positions.

I'd read about pioneering women who had faced blatant

discrimination, where men loudly stated that women were 'unsexed' by men's work and that thinking too much withered their wombs. In the past they had been told they were too plain for certain jobs, or too distractingly pretty. Those who wanted to be architects were told **"women can't climb ladders"** or they couldn't be hired because there were no ladies' toilets. In my grandparents' generation if you were in the professions, you were not allowed to work after marriage. Yes, <u>not</u> allowed to work if you were married no matter how good you were. Not that any of my ancestors had ever reached the exulted heights of 'the professions'.

I had faced a lifetime of pressure to become the socially constructed idea of what a woman should be regardless of my innate talents, abilities or ambitions. John Stuart Mill asserted that women have been coaxed, cajoled, shoved and squashed into a series of feminine contortions for many centuries and I think that's largely true.

But the media and business commentators as well as the dominating male hierarchy were adamant that a working environment saturated with masculinity was fast disappearing and I was now in a post-feminist world where discrimination had vanished, and nothing stands in my way if I'm suitably qualified. This was summed up succinctly by that nice man Stuart Rose, the former Chairman and Chief Executive of Marks & Spencer:

" ... there really are no glass ceilings despite the fact that some of you moan about it all the time ... You've got a woman fighter pilot who went on to join the Red Arrows ... I mean what else do you want for God's sake? Women astronauts. Women miners. Women dentists. Women doctors. Women managing directors. What is it you haven't got?"

That nice man Stuart Rose

A world free of business people like Mr. Rose possibly? The fact that he has had to put 'women' in front of all those professions should have alerted him to the problem, but there again I'm pretty sure he couldn't care less. He should check out the somehow inspiring video that shows that primary school children still believe in male and female job roles even though it was filmed in 2016 (*Inspiring the Future - Redraw the Balance*). ·

Perhaps I should be more respectful of Rose's credentials. He inherited M&S when it had profits of £763 million a year. It hit £1 billion profits at one point but six years later when he retired, profits were down to £604 million. When he took over, he knew that they'd need to attract new and younger customers to survive in the long term. He publicly stated his aim was to make the stores a firm favourite with 35- to 50-year olds, but in the end 75 percent of shoppers in the food halls were over 45 and 65 percent of its clothes shoppers over 55. He didn't achieve what he set out to do then. Not by any means. He did get an £8.1 million golden goodbye gift when he left though.

His disdain for women and equality was demonstrated by making himself both Chairman <u>and</u> Chief executive of M&S in 2008 which broke City rules. Apparently, no one else was interviewed for the job of Chairman. Combining the two most powerful positions in a company contravenes corporate governance guidelines and quite rightly annoyed shareholders. But there again it means no one at executive level or on the board can really disagree with you. As one City player observed at the time: **"His record isn't actually that good if you look back."** Maureen Hilton a retail analyst for Verdict commented: **"When you look at what happened in the end, Stuart Rose didn't do such a great job."** Another analyst, Tony Shiret at Credit Suisse added:

"Rose is getting rewarded just as his strategies are showing signs of failing. The capital spending levels are just astronomical at M&S now. There is significant over-expansion of space as a result, and the company is focused too much on low-price products where it has no heritage. It won't help having Rose surrounded by yes men."

Rose's response to throwing out good governance and

making sure all power was concentrated in his own very masculine hands: **"It's not as if I'm Pol Pot here, going round and chopping off heads."** Helpful explanation.

M&S are now closing hundreds of stores and that was before covid. Some of the kindlier business commentators put this legacy down to **"strategic missteps."** None of this has dimmed his Kanye West style arrogance and unbelievably the government appointed him to examine the organisational culture of under-performing NHS hospitals in 2014.

But what is culture, a workplace culture that is? Culture equals the organisation's collective stories, routines and rituals. It's the total sum of the internal and external branding which includes the shared values and behaviours that everyone knows and subscribes to. It's clarity in roles, an understanding and acceptance of the control systems. To me it's also the commitment to the team, fun, purpose, mutual respect and accountability.

With that definition, then asking Stuart Rose to examine a workplace culture and make recommendations is literally unbelievable. I wonder if they remember his very public comment that: **"Apart from the fact that you've (women) got more equality than you ever can deal with . . . there are really no glass ceilings."** More equality than we can deal with? Is it actually possible to say anything more condescending and dismissive than that? God, it makes me angry.

Mr. Rose's inequality blindness was rewarded by being invested as a Lord in 2008 and Frederick Anderson Goodwin, the former CEO of the Royal Bank of Scotland Group (RBS) was made a 'sir' some four years before. Yes, for a time he was Sir Fred Goodwin, until Britain's Honours

Forfeiture Committee decided in early 2012 to admit him to an even more exclusive club. That of ex-sirs alongside Robert Mugabe and Nicolae Ceausescu.

Ewan Brown who is not just a writer or theorist but has a wide and genuinely impressive 50-year career across the public and private sector, recently wrote a book called *Corporate Ego*. Along with his formidable practical experience he investigated a number of big corporate failures and came up with his own theories. In his view it is mostly the fact that policies have **"no proper challenge and informed criticism"**, allied to wilful chief executives with **"inflated self-confidence"** who were rarely confronted until it was too late. I agree, because the checks and balances that should be there to 'stress test' strategies have gone walkies.

"What need we fear . . . when none can call our power to account?" This could have been said by Goodwin or Rose but was in fact Shakespeare's Lady Macbeth over 400 years ago. In this context of nobody calling his power to account, Goodwin spent £350 million on a new HQ just outside Edinburgh with his own penthouse office being 65 feet ((20 metres) long. I wonder how many key executives were ashamed and embarrassed by this but dare not utter a word. He was so obsessed with global expansion unhindered by his board, he led RBS to a £24.1 billion loss in 2008, the biggest in corporate history. More importantly, 9,000 people, through no fault of their own, went on to lose their jobs.

He inherited a share price of £4.42 when he arrived. It was 66p the day he left. Despite his incompetence and obvious hubris, he wasn't dismissed because he was allowed to take early retirement instead as the RBS internal enquiry into his conduct found no wrongdoing. Really? This is a pretty good body swerve as it means he got to receive an annual pension of £342,500 after he took out a tax-free lump sum of £2.7 million. It would have been considerably less if he had been sacked. Naturally, you and I are paying for Goodwin's comfortable retirement, because RBS received £45 billion of public money to bail it out. As of the end of 2021, we all still own 62 percent between us.

Goodwin is said to have clinically wielded cruelty and created a culture of fear in order to pursue his strategies unchallenged. He didn't seem able to fully grasp the risks his bank was taking or how dangerously thin its cushion of capital. When there is absolute power, good people underneath will try to tell you the issues, but in this type of culture their opinion will be furiously dismissed and worse. Just like Prince Andrew who allegedly told his concerned advisers to **"fuck off out of my office"**, when they said he may want to reconsider his links with convicted paedophile Jeffrey Epstein.

Even on the eve of the bank's collapse, Mr Goodwin simply could not fathom the peril his institution faced. After asking the government for help running into tens of billions, he made little effort to express his thanks. **"He is like a little boy who never admits mistakes"** a former member of his management team is quoted as saying. It reminds me of the often-used media description of Trump as the 'Toddler in Chief'. They're so arrogant and contemptuous of people underneath them and often use temper tantrums to terrorise.

Enter The Right Honourable Liam Byrne MP. In the same year that RBS was bailed out, he arrived as the newly appointed Minister for the Cabinet Office. His way of showing who's boss from day one, resulted in exhaustive instructions to his civil servants (as laid out in an 11-page document called *Working with Liam Byrne)*. It was so absurd it was leaked to the press. Would you ever, in your most confident of moments, write a document with your own name in the title, as if you are a third person to yourself? It's very Shirley Bassey. She might possibly get away with being a diva after 50 years of international superstardom, but not a 38-year-old bald MP totally lacking in empathy.

If you work for loveable Liam you need to remember that **"the room should be cleared before I arrive in the morning. I like the papers set out in the office before I get in. The whiteboards should be cleared. If I see things that are not of acceptable quality, I will blame you."** Furthermore, Byrne insisted that briefing notes should be in 16-point type and occupy just one sheet of paper. **"Never, put anything to me unless you understand it and can explain it to me in 60 seconds."** The Iraq situation, conflict in Beirut, liquidity and the Libor rate, had to be reduced to Janet and John simplicity otherwise it won't pass the Liam test.

When world politics are just too taxing you shouldn't forget his little personal needs: **"I'm addicted to coffee. I like a cappuccino when I come in, an espresso at 3pm and soup at 12.30-1pm."** If you had the utter misfortune to be a civil servant in Mr Byrne's office, at least you only had to put up with him four days a week, because he explains that he does not take Ministerial red boxes home and expects to be at his Birmingham house by Thursday night. Also, you won't have to work on many speeches as they are a **"huge burden, so we don't do lots"**, and as a public servant in charge of the country's finances, for goodness sake **"never rely on me looking at text/ emails."** My favourite bit of the document is the stunning contradiction where he insists that if you present him with anything written it must **"eliminate absolutely, positively all extraneous words."** Obviously, being a twat, he couldn't see the irony in that statement.

Once the manual had been leaked, a spokesman for the minister mischievously responded: **"He is a highly efficient minister but has become more flexible since then. Some days he has his soup at 1.30pm."** When labour got kicked out of office, he lost that job but resurfaced in 2021 as their candidate for West Midlands mayor. He doesn't appear to have gained any humility, as in an interview with Sophy Ridge of *Sky News* he declared he would beat (his opponent) Andy Street easily. Thankfully he lost that election and Mr Street, the incumbent, increased his majority by some margin. Not sure what the 'eager diva', as *The Guardian* described him, is doing now and I really don't care.

These guys are undeniably clever and hardworking (probably not Trump and possibly not Byrne either now I come to think about it) but their personal management styles are lamentable. There are women who act like this too of course, but there are far fewer of them. Their technical abilities get them to the top but only in cultures where total arrogance and bullying of lesser mortals is seen as a prerequisite for success. As they rise to the surface treading on anyone in their way, they become all powerful and lose the plot, but by this time no-one can reign them in. They need to be balanced out. We need technically skilled people but within a structure that plays to their innate abilities and to all those around them, ideally inside a respectful culture that actively allows constructive challenge. As Charlie Chaplin once said: **"Judge a man not by how he treats his equals, but by how he treats his inferiors."**

In Malcolm Gladwell's book *Outliers*, he examines the circumstances behind the 1997 Korean Air Flight 801 which crashed into a hill while on approach to an airport in Guam. 223 people were killed. Korean Air was the country's largest carrier in the 1980s and 1990s but had a poor safety record including several fatal crashes. Gladwell believes **"they were struggling with a cultural legacy, that Korean culture is hierarchical . . . You are obliged to be deferential toward your elders and superiors in a way that would be unimaginable in the U.S."**

He goes on to point out that such a culture is dangerous when it comes to modern airplanes, because such sophisticated machines are designed to be piloted by a crew that works together as a team of equals. They need to be unafraid to point out mistakes or disagree with a captain. According to Gladwell, the co-pilot was afraid to question the poor judgment of the pilot - a fatal mistake.

Similarly, in January 1986 the US Space Shuttle *Challenger* exploded just after take-off. The disaster killed all seven crew members and was blamed on a failed O-ring seal on the shuttle's rocket booster. In February 2003 the US Shuttle *Columbia* was destroyed on re-entry into the earth's atmosphere, again killing all seven crew members. According to anecdotal evidence these fourteen people died unnecessarily because of the culture in NASA's workplace. The senior managers did not actively embrace the idea of constructive challenge. They were happy with their domineering style which encouraged staff to passively agree with their views or say nothing. The following is an exchange between one of the disaster investigators and the Chair of the mission management team:

Investigator: **"As a manager, how do you seek out dissenting opinions?"**
Chair: **"Well, when I hear about them . . ."**
Investigator: **"By their very nature, you may not have heard about them . . . what techniques do you use to get them?"**
Chair: (no answer)

In the case of the *Columbia* tragedy, managers ignored, or more likely, never got to hear, about staff requests to check potential damage areas of the Shuttle using satellites. With *Challenger*, middle managers ignored engineers who warned it was too cold to take off, and that this might cause the o-rings to fail. Senior executives did not encourage and seek alternative opinions that could be critically assessed and evaluated. These events resulted in the tragic deaths of 14 people because of the prevalent workplace culture. I would also add, that to embrace constructive challenge you need a diversified workforce that looks at issues from different perspectives.

Although the facts now undeniably show that women make up nearly two thirds of the workforce in Europe, are better educated and better qualified (60 percent are university graduates) and with more spending power (80 percent of purchasing decisions), there is still reticence to have women at the highest levels of organisations. And yet, figures unequivocally show that companies with women on the board perform better, are less prone to risky decision making, produce more sustainable profits, better staff retention etc etc.

Five years ago, McKinsey demonstrated that gender balanced boards are more successful than mono-cultural boards on every level. Of the 366 companies researched, they found that those in the top quartile for ethnic and racial diversity in management were 35 percent more likely, and those in the top quartile for gender diversity were 15 percent more likely, to have returns above the industry mean.

In a global analysis of 2,400 companies conducted by Credit Suisse, organisations with at least one female board member yielded higher return on equity and higher net income growth than those that did not have any women on the board. You cannot pretend that white men are better at work – you just can't. That's the big change for me, not having to argue that a diversified workforce (not just male/female, but truly diversified) makes business sense, because you can't find any statistics or proven facts anywhere that will disagree with you, despite antediluvian businessmen ignoring them.

Is Rose, the man who is such an expert on inclusive culture, right that everything's equal now? Well no, not even close. As of 2021, men represent:

- 96 percent of the CEOs of FTSE 250 companies
- 90 percent of leaders in the tech sector and 79 percent of IT technicians which has remained unchanged since 2015
- 89 percent of FTSE 250 executive directors
- 89 percent of engineers
- 78 percent members in the cabinet
- 76 percent of university vice chancellors despite the fact that 54 percent of HE students are female
- 75 percent of NHS consultants even though the NHS is overwhelmingly staffed by women
- 72 percent of university professors which is up just 1 percent since 2012
- 71 percent of architects
- 66 percent of MPs

In addition, only 8 out of 22 chief editors of national newspapers and 2 out of 12 supreme court judges are women. 6 out of 23 permanent secretaries head civil service government departments although 54 percent of civil servants are women. There are several high-profile jobs in government that have never been held by a woman including Permanent Secretary at HM Treasury, at the Cabinet Office and at the Ministry of Defence and the roles of Cabinet Secretary and Principal Private Secretary to the Prime Minister. For national security there has never been a woman National Security Adviser or a woman leading the Joint Intelligence Committee or MI6 or GCHQ.

It's unlikely to get better because women are marginalised from conversations on how to solve it. Men at the top are trying to work out how to get more women into similar positions, well some are, but if women are not sitting beside them and not allowed to speak how can they respond to it and formulate a plan?

In all honesty, I wouldn't want any of my female friends or relatives to work in some of these sectors at the moment, most particularly the police. There are numerous recent reports of officers all over the country routinely exchanging racist, homophobic and misogynistic messages with their colleagues. If this is a reflection of their true feelings, are they treating people that are not white, male and straight, fairly and without prejudice on a day-to-day basis? Of course not. I wouldn't want to be in that environment. I guess if it's not for women prepared to go in and challenge it, it's unlikely to change anytime soon.

Female cadets at the Sandhurst military academy have reported that male training officers routinely described all women in the army as sluts. They were often known as STPs meaning 'squat to piss'. A disturbing number of allegations concerning 'conduct and culture' in the army, led Ben Wallace (the Defence Secretary), to summon the army board in late 2021. He had become so exasperated at the prevailing culture that he was calling in top army generals for a dressing down.

In November the previous year he took the unusual step of lifting a gagging order to allow servicewomen to give evidence to a defence select sub-committee inquiry into abuses of power in the military. The inquiry received written testimony from an unprecedented 4,000 women. 64 percent of female veterans and 58 percent of those women currently serving had experienced bullying, harassment and discrimination. Of those that were brave enough to report what happened, which was a ridiculously low number, a third of them said the experience was **"extremely poor."**

Internally, MoD figures show reports of sexual assaults in a three-year period numbered 1,287. During this time 5 men were found guilty of rape in court martials and 50 men found guilty of lesser sexual assaults. The report described the conversion figures from report to conviction as **"astonishingly low."** Yet the Army Cadet Force seems to have a different culture with 34% of cadets and 30% of volunteers being female. They have the 'Step Change' diversity and inclusion project and it really is one of the country's most successful youth projects. The army top brass who are struggling to overcome some of their gender issues would do well to consult them to see how they've done it.

Female representation is no better in the corporate world though. The government-backed Hampton-Alexander Review interim report of 2018 called the imbalance on

FTSE company boards as **"shocking"** and one minister branded the excuses of those male board members as **"pitiful"** with another calling it **"appalling."** Among the top excuses heard by the team conducting the review and coming from a range of 350 FTSE chairs and CEOs were:

> **"I don't think women fit comfortably into the board environment."**

> **"There aren't that many women with the right credentials and depth of experience to sit on the board – the issues covered are very complex."**

> **"My other board colleagues wouldn't want to appoint a woman on our board."**

> **"All the 'good' women have already been snapped up."**

> **"We have one woman already on the board, so we are all done – it is someone else's turn."**

> **"I can't just appoint a woman because I want to."**

To me these people are the same as Stonehenge. They're old, they don't move and nobody is certain how they got to be in that position. Sir Philip Hampton leading the review believes that leaders express **"warm words of support, but (are) actually doing very little to appoint women into top jobs or (are) quietly blocking progress."** Not doing anything to improve it, but actually blocking progress.

Perhaps we can rely on the unions that are set up to defend the rights of workers to lead by example. Unite, Britain and Ireland's second largest and probably most powerful trade union with 1.2 million members, describes itself as a campaigning union standing up for equality for all. As of 2020, over 75 percent of its national executive are male. Sigh.

In the tech world, where the average age of employees is relatively young, the figures are depressingly similar. Meta solemnly declares: **"Diversity is core to our business at Meta. It enables us to build better products, make better decisions and help bring the world closer together."** Microsoft claims that: **"diversity + inclusion = success."** But in the latest 2020 Statista Report, women leadership numbers are:

- 33 percent Meta (Facebook)
- 29 percent Apple
- 27 percent Amazon
- 26 percent Google
- 25 percent Microsoft

Let's put this in context. It means that if you attend a leadership meeting at (say) Microsoft and there are twelve of you around the table, only three will be women. You're not going to get yourself heard much, if at all. It's not the actual figures that are depressing though, it's the lack of movement and the fact that they don't let women speak. Apple holds a couple of global events every year and at each one various Apple executives take to the stage. The number of women appearing on stage in these keynotes has always been low. In 2015, Apple only ever had two women on stage, and neither was an Apple employee. In 2016, women got 7 percent of the speaking time and the picture was the same in 2017 when women spoke for approximately 9 of the 126 minutes, yes that's 7 percent of the time again. Thanks guys.

In March 2022 on International Women's Day, Tim Cook CEO had the audacity to tweet how Apple are celebrating **"the women who are charting the course for a more equitable future, and recognize the rising generation of change-makers who follow in their path."** Bull shit – why do you pay Apple female employees in the UK, a median hourly pay 22% lower than men's, and a median bonus pay which is 52% lower than men's then Timbo?

Machine-learning algorithms build complex models based on big data sets and are designed by very clever people who are almost always exclusively men. They now help make decisions from loan applications to cancer diagnosis. In France, they place children in schools. In the US, they influence prison sentences. They can set credit scores and insurance rates and decide the fate of job candidates and university applicants. But these programmes are often unaccountable and decisions are being made 'in the dark' with no explanation of the process:

- In the US it is estimated that 72 percent of recruitment CVs never reach human eyes.
- Researchers at Cornell University found that setting a user's gender to female resulted in them being served fewer ads for high-paying jobs.
- Women are up to 71 percent more likely to be injured in a car accident as seat belts are designed around male crash dummies.
- The New York Committee for Occupational Safety and Health notes that "standard hand tools like wrenches tend to be too large for women's hands to grip

tightly".

- When Apple launched Siri, users in the US found that she (ironically) could find prostitutes and Viagra suppliers, but not abortion providers. Siri could help you if you'd had a heart attack, but if you told her you'd been raped, she replied "I don't know what you mean by 'I was raped.'"
- If you are in the military or police, stab vests don't accom modate female breasts.
- Sat Nav systems often do not recognise higher pitched women's voices, although despite this the male boss of one sat-nav firm suggested that women: **"needed lengthy training"** on his product if only they were **"willing"** to submit to it.

The list is endless and it's because male designers wouldn't think of those things. I am sure most have the best of intentions, but they just have no experience of the female perspective. The best example which makes me full of anger every time I go to a sporting event, the theatre, cinema or a restaurant is the provision of public toilets. Why do I have to queue for ages just to have a wee? It's demeaning and such a waste of time.

There's a 50/50 division of floor space which apparently has been formalised in plumbing codes, that's why. But if a male toilet has both cubicles and urinals, the number of men who can relieve themselves at once is greater than the number of females. The urinal design means more individuals can get in and out without having to open, close and lock doors and then open them again.

Added to this, women take up around 2.3 times as long as men to use the toilet. Is it because we're too slow or plain selfish in taking our time when there is a huge queue outside? Nope. It's because women are more likely to be accompanied by children, as well as disabled and older people whose toilet needs they have to sort out. Or that around 20 percent of women of childbearing age will be on their period at any one time, and therefore need to change a tampon or a sanitary pad. Or that women's clothes take longer to undo.

Women need more trips to the loo too; pregnancy significantly reduces bladder capacity, and women are eight times more likely to suffer from urinary-tract infections which involves more bathroom visits. Also, as we all know, women are more likely than men to wash their hands and to use the hand dryer.

All in all, it takes a complete moron plus decades of gender bias in architecture and design to believe that the current 50/50 floor base provision is fair and reasonable.

It's plain to see that men (and white men in particular), design things from their own perspective, forget to let women speak and choose you for promotion because they recognise you as one of their own. By doing that, they continue to control our unions, armed forces, police, newspapers, big companies, access to justice, the civil service, parliament, our health, public bodies, technology, software development, the internet and the design of our towns and buildings. I can't think of any professional sphere of our lives that they don't still disproportionally dominate. Possibly cleaning? This leads to unintentional (I hope) bias.

Then there is the thorny issue of the gender pay gap. A voluntary measure was introduced in the UK in 2010 encouraging companies to report on their pay gaps, but of course it was far too embarrassing to admit, and the large companies just ignored it. So, a legal requirement was enacted in 2017 where if you didn't publish your results, you would be fined. This rigid approach, where hourly wage and bonus payments has to be publicly revealed, leaves them with nowhere to hide, or does it?

The measure used for this is slightly absurd. If you have a male-orientated, or indeed, female-orientated business such as bricklaying or hairdressing then naturally you will have more men or women who collectively make up a higher percentage of your workforce and therefore you will see an overall disparity. Male CEOs and Chairman have been quick to point this out. That's not necessarily discrimination nor is it illegal but surely the point is to help encourage more diversity across all sectors including those which have a traditionally biased gender balance.

What they should do if they find themselves with a yawning gap, is not bemoan this blunt measure, but realise they're highly likely to have a huge amount of untapped talent and potentially productive-boosting human collateral sitting there right under their noses. They should be working out how to realise this value to the benefit of everyone, not least their bottom line. That's just plain good business even if you don't subscribe to gender equality.

The really exasperating aspect of these reports, is when there is clear institutionalised discrimination where women are receiving less pay for doing exactly the same job at the same level. It's an inexcusable disparity and although that's been illegal since the Equal Pay Act of 1970 (over 50 years ago!), commentators believe that equal pay is not likely to happen for another 215 years. As that is the case, most companies knowingly flout the law in secret, although some have spectacularly burst into the public domain:

- BBC's China Editor, Carrie Gracie, resigned claiming she was paid 50 percent less than her male colleagues performing the same role.
- Tesco's mostly female instore staff have been paid time and a half for working Sunday shifts, while mostly male warehouse workers are paid double time. Tesco faced a £40 billion equal pay legal challenge mounted by its workers.
- The QI television programme host, Sandi Toksvig, revealed that she was paid just 40 percent of the fee of her predecessor Stephen Fry.
- More than half of women make up medical school entrants and yet male doctors are paid on average £10,219 more in basic pay.
- The Bank of England admits paying male employees, 24 percent more than female employees.
- A quarter of companies and public sector bodies have a pay gap of more than 20 percent in favour of men.

In December 2021 the Institute for Fiscal Studies said that the gender pay gap had seen little improvement in the last 25 years even though women were now more likely to be graduates than men. Even at the top you can see pure discrimination at work, with female CEOs of FTSE companies paid 50 percent less than men for example. Why? Why are they paid less? It's so depressing.

There's no such 'law' in the United States. Obama initiated a rule that required government contractors to report their salary data broken down by race and gender. It will come as no surprise that Trump scrapped it when he became President.

Vince Cable, the then leader of the Liberal Democrat party commented: **"If men are doing all the top jobs and**

the women are making the tea, then there's something wrong." Yes, especially when they're better educated and better qualified. It means women are voluntarily or forcibly taking jobs well below their skill level.

I wonder what Sojourner Truth the ex-slave and American campaigner for women's rights would have thought of all this. She made her famous *Ain't I A Woman?* speech in 1851, and I think she would have expected a tad more progress in the ensuing 170 years. Sorry love, we're still nowhere near.

We're not really in a post-feminist world at all and yet we need the balance that women and other minorities in the workplace can give. Violence against women, gender bias design and corporate discrimination are still everywhere you care to look. How do I find a way to put this right or somehow side-step it?

Sojourner Truth campaigning for women's rights in 1851

CHAPTER 8
Dipping a toe in the water

**"We have to fight the longest,
stupidest waste ever seen
on the planet: the
waste of female
intelligence and creativity."**

Elena Farrante

In my opinion it's the shift in intolerance towards workplace sexism and not social sexism that has been the final straw. That's what has fuelled the #timesup campaign. I think I sense a new shift against bosses who are not nice too. That may sound weak and watery but those of us who want to work in an environment that is fair, tolerant and truly meritocratic have had enough of nasty bosses who bully their way to the top. Perhaps we can start a #fuckyou campaign.

I worked for a guy who was a very religious person and a good old fashioned weekly churchgoer. I thought, great, someone who will be honest and true. I can settle in here and find a place where I will love the meritocratic and kind culture. I was shocked because a few weeks in, it became very apparent that he was a complete bastard. Really nasty and vindictive. So, it seemed that this was no indicator of who might or might not be a bully either.

Throughout my life I've struggled to understand the teachings and beliefs of Christianity even though it was foisted on me as a child. In those days you weren't taught about any other religion and my school was a Church of England school, although to this day I'm not exactly sure what that is. Firmly settled in middle age, I now entirely reject the notion of organised religion and increasingly begrudge its hold over society.

I'm not alone. According to YouGov 55 percent of Brits say they do not belong to a particular religion either. That doesn't mean you don't have your own beliefs and morals just that you don't subscribe to a particular religion. As Jeremy Clarkson once wrote: **"I genuinely believe we are born with a moral compass and we don't need it reset every Sunday morning by some weird-beard**

communist in a dress." I don't agree with the last bit (I think he was referring to the previous Archbishop of Canterbury, Rowan Williams) but I know what he means.

When I was younger, I was more inclined to want to fit in. But recently, along with so many other things in my life, that has changed. I now thoroughly begrudge the impact this horrible person had on making my colleagues' lives a misery at work.

I'm a moderate person, appalled by radicalism and extremist thought and action, but aren't most people? Recent clashes between religious factions, coupled with the die-hard support that Trump has among white evangelical Christians makes me want to distance myself from any type of organised religion even more. In fact, the ascendency of Trump was one of the things that inspired me to make the leap to entrepreneur. He likes to describe himself as a shrewd businessman but if you've inherited at least $413 million from your dad, it's easier to make more money from that base and you can survive without any common sense whatsoever.

I thought I could provide a polar opposite business ethic to the twice divorced, 70-something, obese man who has a face so orange you can read by it. You know, the man who remarked that the US would no longer accept refugees from **"shithole countries."** Separated more than 5,400 migrant children from their parents to try to deter them from crossing the southern border, a practice described as **"government sanctioned child abuse"** by experts. Has been consistently dishonest (according to Washington Post fact-checkers, he has made more than 22,000 untrue or inaccurate statements over the course of his presidency. That's about one an hour, which is a lot).

Banned citizens from seven Muslim-majority countries from entering the United States, cutting off Muslim Americans from their families. Deployed tear gas to a group of protesters and reporters outside the White House so that he could go for a walkabout and pose outside a nearby church with a Bible in his hand. The paradox of that is . . . well, what can you say? Pardoned or granted clemency to U.S. service members accused, charged or convicted of war crimes, including one who was described by his fellow SEALS as **"toxic"** and **"freaking evil."**

And been accused by prosecutors of paying 'hush money' payments to a porn actress, as well as being accused of sexual assault and rape, with numerous offensive quotes, especially the one where he described the advantages of being a famous man because: **"I'm automatically attracted to beautiful — I just start kissing them. It's like a magnet. Just kiss. I don't even wait . . . When you're a star, they let you do it. You can do anything. Grab 'em by the pussy. You can do anything."** I won't go on.

After much reading and searching I discovered I was a humanist. So, this can guide my business life as well as my social life. I can start a humanist company.

No scholarly hierarchy to voice arguments on the interpretation of words written centuries ago. There are no rules on what you can and can't eat. On whether you can have sex, smoke, drive a car or what day you must not go to work. In fact, it's very much about what you can do, rather than what you cannot. It's a positive, life-celebrating sort of approach. It's without hierarchy, so there are no fancy-dress uniforms and no badges, or blinging chains of office and no assumption that any other doctrine is inferior than yours.

There's no call to obliterate or convert any 'disbelievers'. Essentially, it's a way of thinking simultaneously modern and yet rooted in our DNA.

My own brand of humanist thinking means I take full responsibility for the consequences of my actions. I seek to live a good life, I don't always manage it but I try really hard. On the simplest level, I strongly believe we should just be kind to each other and do what we can for other people. These don't have to be monumental showy offy big gestures or involve donating sums of money. They can be small and every day – smiling as you walk past someone. Holding a door open, taking time to listen, putting stuff on freecycle, volunteering, carrying someone's bag, offering up your seat or taking your neighbour's bins out (no, scrub that last one, it's a step too far.)

Yet Christianity and other religions, proclaim man as inherently sinful, and that we displease god, so that we need to be saved and repent. It assumes we're bad, which means it encourages us to think badly of, and distrust, our fellow human beings. I reject that. Christianity has dubious credentials and a shameful history that openly supports misogynistic, racist and homophobic attitudes and discriminatory work practices. Their more recent history exposes the priority given to protect the system they've created at all costs rather than see justice carried out for the most shameful in-house child abuse. There's real sin for you.

I'm sure religions were founded initially to try to explain what happens when we die. It's so tempting to believe that when our life is finished there might just be something else. It gives hope. But let's face it, if there wasn't anything before, there won't be afterwards. The trouble is, it's an extraordinarily hard truth to swallow and a devastating realisation.

It's frightening and doesn't offer the comfort of an everlasting afterlife where you meet up with desperately missed, dead friends and family. But when you accept this and begin to come to terms with it, there's an urgent need to find happiness and ensure that every minute has a purpose.

I was developing a growing sense of anger at the unjustness at big institutions being so overtly biased, and so many bullies ruling over us when they really don't deserve it. Right, that's it. I wanted and needed to do something about it myself. Statistically, it looks like I could live to be 85 or so. That's another 30 years. 30 years?! At 55 it is generally considered too late to make life-changing decisions. But surely the opposite is true. I'm embarking on the last chunk of my existence and I don't believe in an afterlife. It's got to be good. The best stretch, now I've done my work of sorting everyone else out, is about me. Unashamedly so. Still seems selfish saying it. The stifling boundaries that have hemmed me in can be knocked down and I can take complete control of my destiny. No excuses.

My children had left home and had finished university, got jobs and were both settled. I know I was earning a lot of money, but I was unhappy at work, with a demanding managing director who got other people to carry out the tough stuff and was making increasingly erratic decisions. She was a fantasist, liar and to be honest not very bright. How do these people get to the top? Groan!

I thought I still had more to offer and hadn't truly fulfilled my potential even though in many people's eyes I would've been deemed as highly successful. I wanted to prove that it wasn't my style or my abilities that had so often held me back and that I could achieve so much more if given the freedom to do so. I understand that being on a six-figure salary is just a dream for some people, but the effort of being moral inside immoral structures and practices is unreasonably stressful and completely unfulfilling.

Sick of working inside such environments dominated by largely bullying behaviours, invisible to those who are mostly white males who inherit that breath-taking privilege, I was going to start my own business. I wanted to prove I could do it as a working-class born woman and I wanted to create a successful and profitable company where all the things I believed in could be put into practice – profit for purpose, being decent and honest as a leader, creating structures that were fair and transparent.

Being fair is not the same as being soft. If you're soft you'll be walked over by everyone else and if you're the boss, your colleagues will just ignore you and do what they want, but if you crush anyone that threatens the status quo you won't succeed either. I took heart from *The Art of Fairness* a book by David Bodanis. In it he wonders if it's possible to be successful in business without being a terrible person. He uses historical case studies and reckons:

"At first it seems obvious that the answer must be no. When a man like Donald Trump was able to be elected President and remain in office, it's impossible to say that good guys always win. Business seems to show us this all the time . . . look fearsome, a bullying tone in the office suggests the speaker has superior authority, or superior knowledge, or just a stunningly superior pedigree . . . (they) learn the further trick of bullying only those below them, while smiling in a knowing yet ever-so-slightly submissive way to those above them – a psychological two-step understood in

nearly every culture – their advancement is nearly guaranteed."

He goes on to say: **"The logic appears to be impeccable. If someone's willing to take a short-cut to get what they want – if they're willing to shout and cheat and steal; if they don't care what it takes – it seems obvious they would triumph over someone who is not going to act that way."**

His book though, goes on to show that this often does NOT work in the long term. Yes, you have to be able to make hard decisions and not shirk them but he persuasively argues that there is a space between being too aggressive and being too soft, a fairer way somewhere in the middle. Success will take longer, but it is humane and sustained. The most fascinating example in the book is the story of a workplace culture that allowed The Empire State Building, the then tallest building in the world, to be constructed in just twenty months.

I'm sure my business wouldn't be that quick to reach fruition, but I could be patient for success to arrive. I could implement flexible working, family friendly practices, a pure meritocracy, paying people above the living wage, paying suppliers on time, having integrity in business dealings, not working above contractual hours, investing time and training in every member of staff, no matter who they were. Having fun too. Trying things but failing fast. I thought I would adopt the Winston Churchill maxim that to succeed I would move from failure to failure with unerring enthusiasm until I got it right.

I also thought I would use Timpson's as a model for good business. They're the people who do key cutting, shoe and watch repairs. They have 2,155 outlets in the UK and

Ireland. Its family owned, highly profitable and James Timpson has been the CEO since 2002. They run the business using 'Upside Down Management' which was pioneered by his dad, Sir John Timpson. It's a culture based on trust and kindness where everyone is equal. James believes his role is to make sure his colleagues are happy in their jobs because it's plain good business. To do this there are various benefits such as a final salary pension scheme (very rare now), free holiday homes, weekly lotteries and mental health support.

Unsurprisingly, Timpson's has been in the top 10 of the *Sunday Times* '100 Best Companies To Work For' every time it has entered in the last 18 years. James also pioneered the recruitment of ex-offenders, so they now employ over 600 prison leavers (10% or so of the Company). So, it seems it is possible to be fair and kind and make it work.

So that's how I started off, by creating a company with these values. But it's been far from easy doing it all myself, because soon after I started, my husband's aggressive drunken behaviour happened just once too often, and I made the decision that finally I had to leave. Great timing; going through the pain and stress of starting a business and dividing up 32 years of joint finances. I really was going to be very much on my own in this preposterous experiment.

During my teenage years if you wanted a loan or hire purchase, you still needed your husband's or father's signature, and the huge majority of businesses would only get off the ground if they had a male guarantor. This was just a fact. But in this post-feminist world I was sure I could get financial help on my own.

I launched my new company in April 2015. I owned it myself as the 100 percent shareholder and I was the CEO. I couldn't get a loan or even an overdraft facility. I tried loans from invoice factoring services, from the bank, private lenders …. you name it. Banks want to give money to women I am told because their risk profile is better. Well not in my experience. To be fair that might not be because I'm a woman it might be because we were a new small business. Or more likely that because I left my abusive husband, I no longer had a property or tangible assets on which to guarantee a loan – the cash I had in the bank apparently not being relevant.

But research backs up my personal difficulty in securing financial help. Barclays Bank did a survey that showed UK male entrepreneurs are 86 percent more likely to get venture-capital funding and only 9 percent of investment by value is directed at companies that had at least one female founder. This is despite the fact that women entrepreneurs bring in 20 percent more revenue with 50 percent less money invested. Other research by HM Treasury shows that less than 1 percent of venture capital funds were allocated for start-ups run entirely by women. That figure is an utter disgrace and I can't imagine what the excuse is.

If you do get a loan the UK Survey of SME Finances shows that women will be charged more (2.9 percent versus 1.9 percent). Government figures also show that women-owned businesses win less than 5 percent of corporate and public-sector contracts. Getting new business is stacked against you if you're female.

Deloitte estimated that targeted help for female founders could provide a £100 billion boost to the economy over the next 10 years. However, the consistent discrimination against funding female-led companies has remained static for years with no sign of improvement, so that boost is unlikely to happen in my lifetime.

What does this mean practically? Through personal experience it means that after working for 35 years and putting up with all that sexist abuse and physical harassment, I couldn't get funding despite my quite solid business experience. In the end I put my whole life savings in the company which was £350,000. After my rather bruising divorce that left me with £50,000 in the bank if it all went wrong. It was almost everything I had.

To increase my morale, I started reading biographies of successful women who had triumphed against all odds. I found some stunning stories for inspiration. As an example, Hannah Snell who was born in 1723 was abandoned by her husband when she was pregnant. Their daughter died aged just 12 months and she found herself completely alone. He must have been a nice bloke because she learned later that he'd been executed for murder. She always wanted to be a soldier, so in 1745 she disguised herself as a man and moved to Portsmouth to join the marines. She sailed to India and fought in the battle of Devicottail where she was wounded in the leg 11 times. She was also shot in the groin and, to avoid revealing her gender, instructed a local woman to take out the bullet instead of being tended by the regimental surgeon.

In 1750, her unit returned to Britain and travelled from Portsmouth to London, where she revealed that she was a woman to her shipmates. She was honourably discharged and managed to get the navy to grant her a pension for the rest of her life. That was a feat in itself. She then met and married a good guy called Richard and had two children. A happy ending!!

Then there is the inspiring Ruth Charlotte Ellis who

incredibly lived for the whole of the 20th century, being born in 1899 and leaving us in the year 2000. She was the youngest of four children and the only daughter. Her mother died when she was a teenager, while her father was originally born a slave. Ellis came out as a lesbian in 1915 which was an astonishingly brave thing to do then. Although fewer than seven percent of African Americans graduated from high school, she did so in 1919. I can't even imagine the crap she must've put up with as a woman, a black woman and a gay black woman at that.

She worked in a printing company until opening her own press operation from home with her partner Ceciline Franklin. Their home soon served as a refuge for African American gays and lesbians. Using their earnings they supported those who needed books, food or assistance with college tuition. There is now a Ruth Ellis Center which is one of only four agencies in the US dedicated to homeless LGBT young adults. Among their amenities are a drop-in centre, street outreach program, foster care home and a service that provides medical and mental health care. Ellis died in her sleep. Legend. Why do these women not get a higher profile? I had to search them out.

Like Wangaari Mathaai, who was brought up in a village in the middle of Kenya and fought to get schooled, eventually winning a scholarship to study in America. On her return she was denied a job as a lecturer at a university because she was female so went to Germany to continue her studies. She returned as the first woman in East and Central Africa to become a Doctor of Philosophy (1971).

She founded the Green Belt Movement and became the first black woman to be awarded the Nobel Peace Prize. Wangaari developed the idea that village women could improve their environment and also get an important free fuel source by planting trees. She died in 2011 but it's estimated that at least 30 million trees have been planted through her project. Then there's Helen Bamber, Rosa Parks, Maya Angelou, Valentina Tereshkova, Jayaben Desai and:

- Helen Keller – born in 1880 she lost her hearing and sight as a toddler but defied all expectations and got a bachelor's degree. She became a prominent writer and advocate for disability rights.
- Bessie Coleman – started life working in the cotton fields in Texas but dreamed of being a pilot. Prevented from holding a pilot's licence in the US due to the fact she was a woman and black, (not a good combo in the early 1920s), she moved to France and got it there instead. She then became a high-profile pilot flying in notoriously dangerous air shows back in the US.
- Marie Curie – couldn't originally attend University in Poland because she was a woman, so like Bessie, she moved to France and got educated there instead. She went on to become a two-time Nobel prize-winning scientist.
- Ella Fitzgerald – was fifteen when her mother died from injuries sustained in a car crash and then went to live with her aunt in Harlem. She worked as a look out for a brothel, a runner for a Mafia organisation and also earned money singing on the streets until the authorities placed her in an orphanage. Fast forward and despite this traumatic childhood she became known as The First Lady of Song and The Queen of Jazz.

Well, if they can achieve those awesome things with far more barriers than I've faced, surely I could achieve the moderate ambition to run a successful business. I could then hopefully sell it to realise the initial investment, get enough money for my own comfortable pension, buy myself a house instead of renting, perhaps I might have grandchildren by then and, you never know, meet some nice new chap and settle down with him. I love happy endings.

On the downside if the company failed, I would be nearing 60 with literally nothing left except £50,000 in cash after a lifetime of working. Certainly, I wouldn't have a nice chunky public-sector or corporate pension to fall back on. Why would anyone in their right mind start a business from scratch with all their savings, male but especially female? Because in my case, I wanted to prove that it could be done in a very particular way.

I wanted to show the bullies and the old school, white, privileged, educated, middle-aged men that there is a different model. It seemed to me that business has changed beyond all recognition in the last ten years. Competences and not experience are what count. Frankly, experience is not as relevant in many professions as it used to be, because literally everything has changed and continues to do so with frightening speed.

I was fuelled by so much anger at the old world order not being relevant any more. The pace of change was driving innovation and developing new business landscapes and yet the media were still trotting out the same male role models when it comes to what they deem as an 'entrepreneur'. Lord Stuart Rose (and you know what I think of him), Sir Alan Sugar (hardly comparable to Steve Jobs or Bill Gates), Sir Philip Green (although understandably they've gone off him) and Sir Martin Sorrell. They report on their latest business figures and await their business guru advice with bated breath. Programmes are made about them or they front dreadful tv series like *The Apprentice* (Sugar and Trump) where humiliating contestants and encouraging back stabbing and arrogant behaviour is rewarded. This is not how successful businesses should be run. It's irresponsible to keep perpetuating it.

All are horrible macho examples of business bosses which bear no resemblance to the style I prefer, which is inspiring and motivating your employees through support and respect. But many will say, their style does work because the business world is cut-throat and you have to be hard and egotistical to drive your business to financial success. Well, let's see . . . .

Sir Martin, famously founded the WPP Group. It had to be rescued twice in 1992. The shares fell from 570p in 1987 to 50p five years later. It eventually recovered, and he went on a big global acquisition spree, which saw the shares double from their previous high. Impressive? Not to me. It took him 30 years to double the share price he inherited. You probably could have just left your money in a post office savings account to get a better return, but then in the last few years Sir Martin wouldn't have been able to extract cash and shares to the value of £200 million for himself. If you had invested £100,000 in my company from the beginning you would have got back £1 million five years later.

He finally left under a cloud of alleged harassment and bullying claims, accused of using company cash to pay for a prostitute and claim expenses for his wife. That's even-handed of him. One WPP employee said: **"It's a little shocking, but it feels like comeuppance."** Some media commentators say that WPP faces a bleak future, especially having recently paid $19 million to resolve charges that it breached corruption regulations by allegedly offering bribes in India, **"unjustified"** payments in China and **"improper payments"** in relation to government contracts in Brazil among others. This was during Mr Sorrell's tenure.

The company states that the new leadership has now adopted **"robust new compliance measures and controls"** and has **"fundamentally changed its approach . . . and terminated those involved in misconduct."** Still, they paid him £19 million to leave instead of going for gross misconduct. Because, as the new WPP boss put it: **"We didn't want him to throw his toys out of the pram."** He now writes occasional columns in the business press, imparting his wisdom to us lesser mortals.

Sir Alan is famous as the man behind Amstrad which made cheap computers, hi-fis and cigarette lighters. In the 1980's it was said to be worth £1 billion. This was a real self-made achievement – bloody brilliant. However, by 2007 it had dramatically fallen from grace and he sold it for £125 million. That's an 87.5 percent fall in value. He now makes his money from being on the telly and his extensive property portfolio.

Sir Philip is renowned for selling BHS for £1 in 2015, just before it posted debts of £1.3 billion a year later. But my favourite is how he paid his family £1.2 billion in 2005, which was funded by a loan taken out by his wife's company (Arcadia). The same company has been criticised for how it treats its workers, with a number of television programmes (most notably Channel 4's *Dispatches*) claiming he was paying workers less than half the national minimum wage. Now there's a big media frenzy over his alleged systematic bullying and harassment of female staff and his

The media's favourite business gurus – spot the difference

racist attitude. So I don't think their styles work in the long term. Not in the 2020s anyhow.

Research shows that eventually, absolute authority and over confidence leads to more rigid and stereotyped thinking. You airbrush out the bad decisions and wrong turns and you tend to fall back on your simplified reconstructed memories of previous experience. If you stay in that role for a very long period of time, it's almost impossible to critically self-evaluate; you don't make the continuous but small adjustments needed to your operating behaviour and your decision making. You stop listening. So, you don't hear when someone has a better idea or solution than you. The subtlety of situations get lost and the changes in the macro-environment go unnoticed. You then get into a position where you recycle what made you successful in the past. Well, why wouldn't you, it's worked so far?

All that's fine until the context or the culture has shifted so much it bears little resemblance to when you were a real success. When everything is a repeat of what went before your experience is worth something, but not when the landscape has changed beyond recognition. People with long held power are usually older white men at this point in the history of business and politics. They're used to being obeyed and ruthlessly oppose those that challenge. In my opinion they have change blindness as well as inequality blindness.

Not only have they missed the tectonic plates of culture, society and business shifting all around them, even when you point it out they can't see it because they're inside a carefully constructed bubble where nothing that opposes their view is allowed. A classic example comes from somebody who worked for Philip Green: **"Ten years ago, Philip was still going around saying 'who the fuck is going to buy clothes based off a picture on a computer?' He just didn't get it."** Well, there you go.

It follows then, that the longer you're in power whether male or female, the ability to judge yourself gets steadily worse. You get less and less self-aware and so you're no longer able to see that you need to change. Who's going to be brave enough to point that out in the face of someone with super self-confidence and who believes their own publicity?

Aggressive counterattack against anyone stating the facts (Trump is a master at this) and the use of business jargon is their weapon. Despite his carefully constructed 'barrow boy made good' image, Philip Green grew up in a wealthy family and went to an Oxfordshire boarding school. His legendary aggressive personal attacks on detractors deliberately aim to engender inferiority and creates incomprehension and thus self-doubt in the accuser. As Jonathon Meades once put it:

"Jargon begins at the top. It deliberately excludes. It makes sure that people with less education and money can get shafted without knowing . . . . (it is) pompous, delusional and officious. (They) always know best, when really they don't."

So, I was absolutely certain that I would try to grow the company in a short space of time and then leave before I got too big headed and out of touch. I would listen to staff, encourage them to constructively criticise my decision making and set up a working culture that I could be very proud of. It's harder to make money if you're a good person but I'm by no means alone, small business owners across Britain are doing the same thing and slogging away trying to make a better life for their staff and their own families. They're not the media's version of an entrepreneur and they're not trying to do this at the expense of others. They're not wealth creators, they're job creators. They're the backbone of Britain and they're honest heroes. Real ones.

Why does the government always look to the bigger companies for advice on business or place their CEOs and chairmen in advisory roles? Why does the media always seek out these guys for quotes on the economy? What do they know as they sit in their self-important bubbles surrounded by yes men? I would like the media to focus on some decent corporate role models for a change and promote those amazing historical women I managed to unearth. As a little suggestion, I think it would be good to ask down to earth business owners who've done everything the hard way and are really in touch with their employees and what they think. Or maybe, just occasionally, successful self-made women entrepreneurs. Now that would be novel. Here are my suggestions . . .

Dame Stephanie Shirley, who started her own company in the most dreadful adversity, fleeing the Nazis as an unaccompanied Jewish child refugee aged five. She started with £6 in 1962, floated the company in 1993, creating 70 millionaires among her staff and has given over £67 million to charitable causes. Her son had severe autism and tragically died aged 35 following an epileptic fit. She's the most incredible female business leader and philanthropist and should be the most famous businessperson on the planet for how you make things happen by example.

Or Charlotte Tilbury who began as a make-up artist launching her own *YouTube* channel and blog in 2012 which has around 800,000 subscribers. Soon after, she launched her own skincare and makeup range which is now available in the UK, US, Canada, Hong Kong, Singapore, most of Europe, Dubai, Kuwait, Qatar, and 76 other locations. In 2019 she donated £1 million to Women to Women International. She was already working as an ambassador for them to help women learn how to earn and save money, improve their family's health and make their voices heard at home and in their communities. In June 2020, Charlotte announced her partnership with the Spanish fashion and fragrance company Puig, who fought off rival bids from l'Oreal and Unilever to acquire a majority stake in her business. It was said to be worth £1 billion at that point.

Or Sarah Wood, a Cambridge graduate, with a first in English and a PhD. She set up a tech company, Unruly, in London with two partners in 2006. The company has since grown from a start-up into a multi-million buyout, when nine years later News Corp bought it for £58 million. There are now 300 employees and new offices in Tokyo, Melbourne and India. Sarah strongly believes that women should feature more prominently in tech businesses instead of the current industry norm of 17 percent. In her company, females make up 44 per cent of the Unruly board, 46 percent of managers and 48 percent of the total workforce. So it can be done!

Or Renée Elliott, the co-founder of the UK's first organic supermarket, Planet Organic, way back in 1995. Its mission was, and still is, to promote health in the local community. It took a huge amount of effort to get it to fly but when it did her business partner decided he wanted it all to himself and tried to oust her. They were in litigation for 14 months and the High Court trial lasted 11 days with legal bills reaching £560,000. She described it as **"exhausting and frightening"**, but she won and although she has sold a stake to Inverleith, she runs it with her husband. They have recently taken over As Nature Intended which is giving them an even bigger reach into local communities.

Or Robyn Fenty who was born in a humble bungalow in Barbados but now lives in London on and off. She launched Fenty Cosmetics in 2017 and still owns 50 percent which is valued at £1 billion. She owns the lingerie brand Savage x Fenty with a 30 percent holding which is also said to have a near £1 billion valuation according to *Forbes*. Her Clara Lionel Foundation has donated countless millions to natural disaster response programmes around the world. This includes supporting mobile emergency medical teams, rebuilding hospital infrastructure and providing lifesaving access to medical care in remote areas. You might know her better as Rihanna.

Or Sarah Luxford or Maggie Philbin who are working so hard to get more women into tech. Chrissie Rucker (The White Company), or Kiran Mazumdar-Shaw (Biocon), Anne Boden (Starling Bank) or the mysterious Denice Coates (Bet365). They all have incredible expertise in their own spheres. I would love to know their perspectives on business, entrepreneurship and the economy, but they rarely, if ever, get asked. They're all invisible when it comes to the business press.

I remember going to a female business event where Theresa May was speaking when she was Home Secretary. Whatever you think of her politics, at that point she had risen to one of the top jobs in government as a woman and would soon become prime minister. She talked for a while on the ridiculous pressure and enormity of the role with her usual modest, cautious and measured tone. Then someone in the audience asked what it FELT like when newspapers like the *Daily Mail* ran a double page spread on her lack of dress sense, choosing the frumpiest photos they could find amongst hundreds of thousands that had been taken of her over the years. She said it really, really hurt and that it always knocks your confidence, but her husband was a great support and helped her put it in perspective. Her response in essence, was that you just get up the next day and carry on dealing with the very difficult things that are on your desk that morning. Why did she have to go through this, as if the job is not bloody hard enough as it is?

Anyhow, I've made up my mind to join the invisible small business heroes and start a humanist company inspired by some incredible invisible historical women with a distinctive culture based on respect. Yes. I'm going to chuck in my job, use my life savings and give it a go. Now, how do I combat the discrimination that will derail my ambitions?

CHAPTER 9
Sink or swim

**"Everyone has a plan until
they get punched in the mouth."**

Mike Tyson

It's early 2015 and this is my plan.

You don't have to look too hard to see that the UK education system was built for the industrial revolution and not for the 21st century. School is not relevant in a digital/ AI/deep learning and soon to be 'quantum' age. It has a very narrow set of things that are measured. Change, emotional intelligence, communication skills, creativity, flexibility and other forms of intelligence are not taught or measured but as an employer these are what I need.

After 35 years it's the first time that I really feel my inherent skills are suited to the modern business world. I know too, that there are lots of people out there like me, but they haven't been given some of the breaks I have. How could I attract the right people to my new business? How do I spot the racists, bullies and sexists so I can exclude them? I thought it might be quite difficult especially as I really don't care if someone has an A level in geography and can tell me the capital city of Belarus, (which by the way, I can look up on my phone in a nano second). It doesn't tell me anything, other than they might be less likely to get lost on the way to visit a client.

How do you recruit for success? Who are these people? How do you attract them to your business?

If you want the best innovators you need to stand out and you need to stand for something. A strong sense of purpose and a strong culture needs to be 100 percent aligned to strategy, not just platitudes. The best story wins – as long as it's authentic. I wanted a strong culture that allows innovation and celebrates it and most of all is happy with failure but failing quickly. It should genuinely allow people to explore new ideas and crucially, then try them out.

I am a zealous missionary for my ideas but I want my employees to be too – I want them to buy it and believe it 100 percent. If it succeeds, they can repeat it and live it without any reference to me. I wanted to ooze all that culture in our job ads so the right type of people apply. I didn't want to ask for qualifications or references. I couldn't care less what they've done before – it's their behaviours and attitude, ability to embrace change, make suggestions, that I care about.

I wanted to recruit people with a Star Trek mentality i.e. happy to go where no man has gone before. And that is what we would test at interview.

I started with my best friend's daughter, Brady, using two laptops and with a large stash of Yorkshire tea bags. We were both working at an R&D tax relief consultancy but we were unhappy at the way it was being run. We knew if we went on our own, we could reach so many more small businesses and help them gain the funding they needed to thrive and 'breakthrough'. That is why we named it Breakthrough Funding.

We began trading in April 2015. Together we wrote the content for the website, designed the process systems in detail from scratch, developed the specification for the IT infrastructure, commissioned the client contracts and we even agreed on what colour bins we fancied in a 'proper' office when we got that far. In the first month we had zero income, but that was to be expected.

Even so, the proper office was acquired just three months later, along with our first staff appointments including Daisy, an incredibly bright dental receptionist who had never been given a chance to shine at school given that her dad was in prison and her mum a non-functioning alcoholic and Dan, a window specialist (don't ask). Since then, the team have been helping small companies grow into great big ones by accessing the valuable government incentive imaginatively called 'R&D tax relief' designed to help nurture innovation. We already knew a lot about the scheme, especially Brady, but we delved even deeper and taught ourselves everything about this slightly complicated tax arrangement. We wanted to reach out to as many small business owners as possible, guiding them to access this fund so that it helps their cashflow and their growth.

None of us are accountants, and aside from my MBA, we didn't have any financial qualifications. But as I said it's not experience or qualifications that we thought mattered but the ability to learn and apply other natural abilities. We believed that these latently reside in people who want to work somewhere that would value them for what they were. Education is 'done' to people to pass exams that usually have no use to me as an employer. It's often of no use to the student either because it's a passive process which limits people and therefore stunts their ability to innovate. Many people think they're a failure because they failed their exams at school in one small period of their life when anything could have been going on that distracted them from their studies. Covid for example. This makes no sense at all.

So why would you employ people who have great exam results and what does it tell you? As the wonderful, wonderful Hans Rosling explained in the best TED Talk ever - if you do a multiple-choice quiz and you were to put the correct answers on a banana, a chimpanzee will choose the answer to questions correctly 50 percent of the time by pure chance. So, they will score five out of ten. A highly educated student will do much worse than that. In Rosling's research they got the equivalent of three and a half out of ten correct. As he said: **"I had shown that top Swedish students know statistically significantly less about the world than the chimpanzee."** Why? Because too often it's not ignorance or lack of formal education that makes you choose a wrong answer but pre-conceived ideas.

I believe that these obviously talented students, then get hired and forced to work in silos, play petty office politics, understand they must be risk averse, work long hours, are burdened with admin, a blame culture and a lack of joy. You don't find innovation there and that culture doesn't allow for judicial risk taking and you make the wrong decisions because of pre-conceptions. It's a risk averse atmosphere that looks to call out those that make mistakes. What a waste.

All our staff are self-taught and self-starters. They have a range of skills which is not about being academically intelligent in the two inches above your eyebrows. We don't care if they have no qualifications. A degree is not the key to being great at customer service or innovation – probably quite the opposite. It's no fault of their own if they didn't go to university and to be honest I don't want them to have gone to university anyway really. We just need people who can think, communicate, innovate, challenge and embrace change. We also decided that if a candidate was technically talented with amazing skills but they weren't a team player and upset everyone else, then they just weren't worth it. It might leave you with a gap, but it would be filled eventually by the right person. As a policy, me and Brady decided we would rather have a hole than an arsehole.

Over the years we have employed an ex-sniper who served in Afghanistan, a zoo keeper who specialised in penguins, a cleaner, a voluntary hospice worker, a property consultant, a car salesman and a window specialist (obviously). We find what they are good at and shape the job around them. We set them up to succeed. We invest and train them and each one has a mentor from outside the business. Most of them have never ever had anyone who was willing to develop their skills with them. We're only as good as our people, so it's common sense. Any type of practical education is helpful – an apprenticeship, qualifications in a trade, coding, hairdressing, but no one thing is better than the other.

Most have held low paid jobs but have still got up in the morning to go to work and they all know what it's like to be talked down to. To be patronised. To go unnoticed. I've been a toilet cleaner, receptionist, barmaid, admin assistant, waitress, you name it, just to earn money to fund my degree education and I've never forgotten what it's like to work long unsociable hours but still be skint.

Disadvantaged people can't usually get a 'professional' job. But if you let them in you can support them and create the right culture. They feel they belong, they help other people belong and they thrive and grow in confidence. They will literally do anything for you. But they need to have lots of energy. Part of the culture we set up is that no one is allowed to work at weekends or after hours or on their holidays. No one can have a laptop to take home to work in the evenings. They get a bit of a telling off if they read emails out of hours. They have to have an hour lunch break and they're not permitted to eat at their desk ever and everyone finishes at lunchtime on Friday. Consequently, we rarely had people off sick and they are fresh, alert and up for it every day.

The only exception to this was myself. You could say that means I was not setting a very good example, but I had to work like an absolute dog in order to make sure we had consistent income and new clients. Being responsible for people's livelihoods is a very serious undertaking. There was another reason too. I would start very early in the morning and then leave work at 7:30pm and go swimming at my local gym when no one was around. I used to pretend that the pool was mine. That I owned it. I let the water wash away the day's stresses and strains as I ploughed my way through the 50 lengths target I always set myself. It also meant I didn't get home until after 9pm every day so I only had one hour of being alone which could be filled by watching *Coronation Street* or a gritty police drama with a glass of ice-cold wine.

As a bonus I lost two and a half stone in a year. Yep, and I've kept it off. It's very, very nice to wear size 10, or depending where you shop, size 12 clothes and I haven't been in that position probably since I was 22. I just fell into cooking Northern boy meals of meat and potatoes, rice or pasta and curries. Too much booze, Walkers and takeaways because I was knackered, and it was what my husband wanted – well that was my excuse.

Then I spent 30 odd years trying to hide my size with carefully chosen camouflage clothes. Now, I eat the things I like, though not the same volume, because my body doesn't want to. Lovely fish, veg, loads of potatoes (love potatoes), Ottolenghi salads and obviously occasional roast lamb, the odd steak and belly pork. Oh yeah, and Sunday roast with Yorkshire puddings.

Weird, that now I don't have to be an archetypal wife and mother I can wear all sorts of fashionable clothes and even a bikini if I want, although there is some pretty saggy skin stuff poking out. I might still have a bit of a jelly belly, but who needs a waist at my age anyhow? Nonetheless, at the age when you least care, you wear whatever you want, whereas when you were younger you were so damn critical you actually looked gorgeous didn't realise it and shied away. Now I think I must've looked pretty damned good at 22. If only I knew. Madness.

Anyhow, keeping very busy was the way to get through all this I thought. And when sometimes I struggled to get up in the morning because of sheer exhaustion or just deep sadness because I was on my own, I would listen to Freddie on Spotify and put my game face on:

"The show must go on.
Inside my heart is breaking.
My makeup may be flaking
but my smile, still, stays on.
I'll face it with a grin.
I'm never giving in.
On with the show."

In my view success is about making mistakes. It's about imagination and freedom. You have to be able to join dots, appreciate outliers, be inquisitive, understand behaviours, look for patterns that are not at first obvious, use qualitative aspects, think in a non-linear way. This is only achievable with people who are a bit different and who can spark off other people who are nothing like them. That's not just about colour or gender, that's not enough. It's about that <u>and</u> age, background, creed etc etc or in modern speak this means a truly diversified workforce. It's the key to success because it embraces diversity of thinking, innovation, challenge, debate and off the wall contributions. If everyone is an A student (i.e. great at passing exams), white, middle class and been on a gap year travelling, they're clever but only in one dimension.

Today, diversity of background and thought is critical to make a company thrive and grow. I wanted to start a company first because I wanted to prove I could do it on my own terms, and secondly to get together the right people to generate innovative and creative ideas that could disrupt current thinking and ways of doing things. I wanted to allow them to stick their head above the parapet and tell me, the boss, when something felt wrong. That's the first step. But so too is the ability to change. Change, and changing fast is the key to creating value.

Maybe in some sectors or forward-thinking companies there honestly is a diverse and meritocratic environment, but as you know it is not what I had experienced. Perhaps you might say, that in the five years that I ran my own company I will have witnessed a change. As a society if we truly want to allow women a clear path to succeed as entrepreneurs the sexist blinkered attitudes have to go. There are many people, mostly men who will say it's not a problem any more just like Mr Rose. Well, they're so wrong.

Here is a just a very small illustration of my post-feminist (haha) business life as founder and CEO of my own business (there are so many to choose from) in recent times:

In 2018 we had a client ring up our office asking to speak to one of our consultants. No one was available, but they were informed that I was in the office and as a director of the company I would be happy to help. The caller asked if there was a man he could talk to at that level and didn't feel in the slightest bit embarrassed about asking that question. He was politely told that I was actually the owner, so I probably would be able to help. He declined to speak to me. He wanted to talk to a man and not a woman.

I go to a lot of business events, dinners, lunches and award celebrations because unfortunately I have to network to get new business, even though I don't like it. I'm still in the minority at most of them. Not a minority 40:60, but a minority 10:90 or 20:80. I've lost count of the number of times a middle-aged white guy at these events has offered me guidance when I didn't ask for it. God it's condescending and patronising. As Dame Stephanie Shirley says: **"Ambitious women have flat heads."** That's because we're always being patted on them, and you can tell when it's just about to happen as they always start by saying **"let me give you some advice ...."**

I've noticed that mostly this type of man has worked in a large bloated corporate up until 10 or 15 years ago. They're now beached on the shores of small business consultancy or coaching, even though they've no experience in this area. They're unemployable. Social media and technology have passed them by but they've self-published a book filled with clip art and some sort of process or system they've invented to take your business step-by-step to success. That's why they feel entitled to give you advice when you haven't asked for it, they've got a system and a crap book to their name with a really dodgy cover design. Often they don't ask what you do and have no concept of your professional prowess or business success because they do 90 percent of the talking, mostly about themselves. They're as useful as Anne Frank's drum kit.

Katy (not her real name) is one of our senior employees. She went to a business networking event at the beginning of last year. We go to a lot of these as I've said, because it's a very good source of new business. Usually you arrive and you don't know anyone. I'm not sure if men feel intimidated in these situations, but it's very intimidating if you're a woman. You know that even now, you'll be hugely outnumbered and the environment, the rules, the culture, it's all male and you're an outsider. Katy has started to go to these in my place, because as we grew, I just couldn't go to them all.

She's been appalled at how she's been treated. I think she thought I was exaggerating about what it's like and even though I've coached her, it's been a real revelation. She's lost count of the number of times she's been addressed as 'luv' or been asked if she 'works' in the office. On one occasion she bent over to collect her name badge at the welcome desk and one of the male networkers groped her breasts pretty hard. This quite rightly is now called sexual abuse. It was witnessed by the woman handing out the badges who was in her late 20s. Katy was shocked and then, which happens all the time, wondered if she really had been groped. You think you would say something loud and cutting, or punch them on the nose, but this is rarely the case, because you're dumb-struck, and then you doubt yourself. Did it just happen, or did I imagine it? She looked back at the woman giving out the badges to sort of verify if it was real, and before Katy said anything, she said: **"Yeah, he does that all the time."**

Whose behaviour was worse? Male networker? Katy? The badge woman? Whatever your thoughts, the outcome will be that he keeps doing it. What he won't know is how it feels to be on the receiving end. Katy won't go to that networking event anymore because she doesn't want to be humiliated again and she's frightened that next time he might corner her alone in the car park or do something even worse.

Similarly, another one of my senior female employees went

147

to a breakfast networking event very recently, let's call her Mandy. She was talking to a male attendee when another man stood in front of her and pointedly stared at her breasts for an exceedingly long time. Eventually, the man next to her said: **"Let's all look at Mandy's tits for ten minutes"**, which was a clumsy attempt to get this attendee to stop this offensive behaviour, although this obviously made her feel ten times worse. Was the staring man embarrassed by this? No. He responded directly to Mandy: **"Well, your badge is in a very inviting area."** She won't attend these particular networking events anymore either. As my duty of care as an employer, should I keep putting my female staff in this position?

The niece of a tax expert friend of mine went for her first post-graduation job interview last year. She's a frighteningly bright, capable young woman with a great cv and experience. At the interview the first question from her potential male boss was: **"What type of girl are you?"** For god's sake.

Just before Christmas 2017 a tech entrepreneur that I met who's in her early 30s went to meet a high-profile PR professional who is now quite elderly. She's incredibly well educated and respected. He'd promised to give her some contacts so that she could promote her business. During the lunch meeting he asked her on three separate occasions if he could touch her breasts. Each time she politely said 'no'. Rightly or wrongly she continued chatting because as a woman she didn't want to cause a scene and after all he was very well known. Needless to say, he didn't give her any contacts and I guess at least he made the concession, in these enlightened times, to ask to touch her breasts, because before #metoo, he probably would've just gone for it.

In 2015, I went to the Federation of Small Businesses National Conference in Birmingham. I wanted to support small businesses and hoped I could help inspire more women to become entrepreneurs. In the lead up, much was made of making the FSB more diverse. I don't recall seeing a single female speaker on the platform either as a guest speaker or on one of the panels. The conference was for two days.

Similarly, I went to an Institute of Directors dinner just after Christmas 2017. Twenty IoD member business owners were invited to discuss how to make the organisation more inclusive. There were just three women at the dinner and no one looked like they were under 45 years of age. They invited a middle-aged former Ireland rugby player that I've never heard of, to give us a talk on leadership in today's cut-throat, multi-lingual, technically enabled, fast-paced business world. I thought we were going to have a good discussion throughout dinner to see how we could get a more ethnically diverse membership with more women and young people involved too, but no, apparently, we needed a speaker, although this was not advertised beforehand.

This guy (the same age as me) then proceeded to give us the benefit of his experience while I was served some manly god-awful meat and potatoes to eat. His hypothesis was based on a book he'd read on leadership that was written in the 1940s. Some incredibly boring and irrelevant 45 minutes later, he explained his key point, the climax to our evening where this final story would lead us to understand the epitome of good leadership …. one of the All Black's team members had sex with a woman, who was not his wife, in a toilet cubicle at the airport on the way home from a rugby tour. Yawn.

The other players, not the management, decided themselves that this behaviour was unacceptable. They banned him from playing for the team for three months. There you are. Apparently, this was the essence of teamwork and leadership because they all agreed and acted in tandem, and we should learn from it. Not a single man around the table thought that this story, the supposed highlight of our dinner, was remotely inappropriate or ironic given why we had been brought together. I left before they started talking about how to make the IoD more inclusive, if indeed, that conversation ever took place. Hopefully, they're actually doing something more practical about it these days.

I don't have a high-pitched voice and I'm quite softly spoken in business situations. That means I get interrupted or talked over by men quite often, as well as being ignored completely if you wish to ask a question at a meeting or in a more public session. As Mary Beard (more of which later) said: **"It is still the case that when listeners hear a female voice, they do not hear a voice that connotes authority; or rather they have not learned how to hear authority in it."** Or as described in Mary Ann Sieghart's book *The Authority Gap* one study found that men thought women were dominating the conversation, even when they spoke for only 30 percent of the time.

You just get used to being passed over or interrupted. In terms of a powerful or experienced businessperson, the mental picture inside most people's head is not a woman. They just can't see or imagine you as that, so they'd rather talk about themselves, cut across you or talk past you to someone that does appear to have that culturally imposed demeanour.

All this is in the last seven years, not in the last century. Sure it was bad in the 1970s when I started getting subjected to sexual harassment but it's still everywhere in business even now. It's no wonder women are abandoning their entrepreneurial dreams and flocking to leave the workplace.

CHAPTER 10
Pond life

"No matter how you feel, get up, dress up and show up."

Regina Brett

Another reason women give up their careers and business is because it's too confrontational. Men are more aggressive and intimidating than women, and not just physically. Often, they don't realise this, but we feel it all the time. On public transport, in meetings, one-to-one discussions, social situations and so on. Most men have no idea at all that this is how women feel nearly every day. They can leverage it if they want, and sometimes do so in business. The threat of it can be used as a weapon, although I've found that it's not often used deliberately. However, a minority are very happy to do so ….

Having launched the business in April 2015, we got our first client that May and then began to gradually rack up our monthly income even though, obviously, we were still making losses. Early on, I was referred by a friend to a motor sport and vehicle business that employs the most brilliant engineers to design and manufacture cutting edge solutions for that sector.

After meeting the two owners, Simon Horrobin and his sidekick Mark, it was evident that we could help them secure government money (it's what we do). They said they were in trouble as the three companies they owned, had outstanding debts with HMRC and they were struggling to meet the payment plan they'd agreed with them. Jobs were at risk. I promised we'd work hard to secure money for their wonderful innovations which would wipe out that debt in each of the companies and give them considerable amounts of cash too. Hopefully this would protect their future in the short term. As a team, we gave this top priority because we wanted to help.

Horrobin duly signed the contract in two places in front of witnesses and we began work. As promised within a couple of months, we had wiped out their HMRC debts and got a healthy six figure sum in cash on top for them. Now, to pay my bill for all the hours we had spent on it. He didn't pay when he was supposed to. That's not unusual, so we went through our credit control process sending letters at specific intervals each getting nearer to legal redress. I would prefer to come to an agreement and keep up communications; a reasonable payment plan or something to help settle, but no response. He wouldn't take my phone calls or answer my numerous emails. Regrettably, and not my favourite option, we started to get solicitors involved.

The trick, which I have now learnt is that some people who are very experienced in non-payment, rarely use a solicitor. This means they're not racking up huge legal bills. They either represent themselves or simply ignore everything that's sent to them, even court orders. This substantially increases the timeframe of non-payment with the end game that your legal fees will escalate alarmingly. You'll spend so much time on collating evidence with your solicitor, getting court orders, preparing for court appearances, appointing bailiffs and so on, that you'll either have gone bust in the meantime or you'll give up. It's taken me a while, but I now know this is a deliberate and well-trodden modus operandi by people who know how this all works; they don't incur costs to resolve the issue, but yours keep mounting.

Bearing in mind my business was just three months old, non-payment was really going to hurt. He knew I was vulnerable. Did he also think that because I was female there might be less chance of me pursuing this distressing course of action? I'm not sure.

If you're not familiar with the legal system it took some 12 months before we edged towards a court hearing, all the while he tantalisingly promised to pay large chunks of the outstanding fee if we could just wait another couple of months. Blah blah. When court looked inevitable, he then declared, using a legally binding witness statement, that he'd not actually signed our contract in two places and that the signatures were counterfeit. The inference of course, was that I forged his handwriting. I'm not sure this is correct, but I think he committed fraud by stating that I'd committed fraud.

It took months using expensive experts to prove that it was indeed his signature, but once that allegation was settled, he then counterclaimed. We were professionally incompetent apparently. We had to find an independent expert to prove that we were not, even though we got him back cash exactly as we said we would, and that our work had been passed by HMRC. The counter claim didn't go anywhere and then at last almost exactly two years later we got a judgement from the District Judge in the county court ordering Horrobin to pay with added interest and our legal costs. He didn't.

Even though the court ordered payment, he just ignored it, so we had to go back to court again. We obtained an order to freeze his company bank accounts (a third-party debt order); a further long drawn-out process. This would legally allow us to seize the money in them, up to the value we were owed. When his bank eventually obliged, there was only £150; he'd cleared them out. We got another court order to send in a High Court Enforcement Officer who can go in and cease equipment and machinery.

I thought it would be like that programme *Can't Pay? We'll take It Away!* where they arrive unannounced and start taking your office chairs away even when you're still sitting on them, but not a bit. When the officer arrived, having let them know he was coming that day (are you supposed to do that?), all the factory gates were closed so he couldn't get in. The next day we went along to see what was going on. They were open again. The HCEO said he wouldn't be bothering again because he thought they didn't own any of it anyway. How did he know that? Very suspicious.

Our only other option was to apply a winding up order to the company (effectively putting it into liquidation). If you think getting a third-party debt order takes time and is stressful, winding up takes even longer. We finally got these orders agreed in court and it was put in the hands of the Official Receiver. This government official then investigates and looks to retrieve any money or assets they can find to pay creditors. By now we've waited nearly three years to be paid.

The reports of the Official Receiver of The Insolvency Service of the High Courts of Justice declared that Horrobin and his co-director had transferred huge sums of money to one of their other companies. This is illegal. They continue to be viscerally silent. They choose to pay nothing even when the law presses them to do so. You don't know you've failed in your latest attempt until you feel the blood running down your back from the latest dagger blow and your solicitor asks for more money to try some other legal tactic.

It's coming up to six years since we issued our invoice and having suffered accusations of forgery and signature fraud and attacks on the professionalism of our business we seem to be no further forward in receiving what we're owed, let alone the huge amounts I have had to pay my solicitor as we go along. In short despite all sorts of 'official' people being involved, he still hasn't paid. It's no wonder that nice people drop out of business. It's stressful and you need nerves of steel and deep pockets. The law or government guidelines are no help and it's all so difficult to navigate.

My personal opinion is that disgusting people like these two guys see paying as optional not an obligation. Women generally hate conflict, argument and aggression. They're proven to be more risk averse than men and prefer mediation and non-confrontational solutions. Up against nasty bullies, we will almost always back down, as will many men. Bastards who don't care about the pain and suffering they inflict know this only too well. Business is rough and bruising no matter what sector or industry you are in. Less women succeed as entrepreneurs or give up in harsh professions because they can't, or won't, stick it out. The law needs to support people who are not paid and woman have to toughen up and take these people on, if they want to succeed.

If you start to pass the £1 million turnover mark, your business is a serious one and legal wrangles become an unfortunate fact of life. Only 4 percent of businesses ever reach this goal, but ours is one of them and we did it, profitably, inside 14 months. Being an ethical employer and having a profit for a purpose, can work. The downside is you start to do business with operators like Horrobin and the man who we describe in our office (ironically) as 'the lovely Kevin'.

I must stress they're not the norm, but you start to come across them periodically, and any business owner will have deep scars if they've managed to survive these encounters, and even worse ones if they haven't. They're quite often responsible for either putting people out of business or forcing them to give up, just like some of the large corporations who deliberately make late payments or stipulate that 120 days is their standard payment term. It's scandalous and it's holding back our economy and natural talent for innovation and entrepreneurship. In my experience, women rarely act like this as a matter of deliberate corporate policy.

The lovely Kevin Dougall was introduced to me by a highly respected director and started working with my company as a consultant. He was genial, avuncular and entirely plausible. Even my corporate lawyer who is utterly brilliant and pretty scary, thought he was a nice guy and she's not easily fooled. For some reason I found myself talking to Kevin about some of the problems I'd encountered while trying to get the business off the ground.

He knew I was in the middle of a divorce, that I was in a battle with Horrobin who at that stage had accused me of forging his signature and our struggles with cash flow. He could see how tired and stressed I was, and he appeared very caring and considerate, which I guess I was flattered by, even though I was not in the least bit attracted to him in any way – fat, balding old guys not really being my type. But I was lonely, so I guess it was good to chat to another business person about how difficult everything seemed.

Less than six months later he set up a rival company and passed it off as mine. He even issued invoices using my company name and VAT number. As you would imagine, I was in shock and felt so stupid to be duped by this man and wondered why, uncharacteristically, I had revealed so much about my situation. I then refused to pay his final consultancy bill because at the very least his company had not performed the services we'd agreed in our contract. In return, personal threats against me having not worked, he tried to wind up my company knowing that my staff would lose their jobs and what that would mean for their families.

Apparently, you're not allowed to wind a company up if there's a genuine dispute, which of course there was. He claimed there was no dispute and went right on ahead anyway. So with a turnover of over £1 million (at that time), and with a disputed non-payment of under £4,000 where he had acted fraudulently and his services had not been performed, he launched into legal action in which I had no choice but to engage. Can someone go ahead and attempt to get your company wound up when there is clearly a dispute, despite what the law says? Yes, they can do that.

I had to rush to get a court injunction to stop the winding up (basically your bank account gets frozen and you can't trade or pay salaries, so it's game over). He still didn't stop. After months of witness statements and rescheduled court appearances because he kept failing to turn up, the judge finally ruled against him because there clearly was a dispute and it wasn't owed to him anyway. My company was saved, and he was ordered to pay legal costs of £22,000. Remember this figure and marvel at how it begins to escalate.

This was over four years ago, and despite the court ruling, you will not be surprised to hear he hasn't paid a penny voluntarily. He put his company into administration which means I can't touch any of his assets. The plain fact is, despite a High Court order, if he defaults, all those solicitors and court fees still need to be paid and the person who he has wronged, has to pay those costs i.e. me. Yep. I didn't know that either. He's in the wrong, a court has ordered him to pay, but if his company doesn't, you have to instead because it's you that employed your legal team not him.

Incredible! So far then, I have to pay £22,000 to my lawyers for him wrongly taking me to court.

We had won against him claiming his unpaid consultancy fee, but not his fraudulent passing off. Having done so much damage to my brand and having extracted money from other people while pretending to represent my company, we had to go to court again to stop him continuing this activity. Reputation is everything and he was beginning to destroy mine. How would I be able to sell a company if its reputation was rubbish? By this time the legal cost alone of going to trial had already amounted to £100,000 on our side. He started threatening me and my daughter (whose name he managed to find) which made me feel vulnerable living in rented accommodation where I usually arrived after work late and in the dark. I guess he was hoping I would back down. I didn't.

During the process for some of the court hearings he simply didn't turn up again so they had to be rescheduled which adds weeks to the process each time. On one of those days he wrote to the court to tell them he had broken his foot, (no sign of that a couple of weeks later), for another hearing that he had severe mental health issues (we asked for a doctor's certificate or something similar, but instead he sent a photo of the tablets he was purportedly taking), another that he had a business meeting that he couldn't miss and on a particularly important hearing that his daughter had a miscarriage that morning (I really do hope that she didn't of course as that would have been absolutely awful, but in the end you don't believe anything he says at all). Each time, we're all sitting there, court bundles prepared, stressed out and the judge orders that another date has to be set. No sanctions are imposed for wasting court time like this and my solicitor's bills have increased again.

It was agreed it would finally go to trial before a judge and it was to be heard at The Royal Courts of Justice in London over four days. Dougall stated that he would be representing himself, a litigant in person, as it's called. This is a masterstroke. He is of the Horrobin school of fuckery. Not only does Dougall not incur his own legal fees, the judge has to give him huge leeway, and my (expensive) barrister has to help him while he cross-examines me because it's bad for my case if he's seen to put the lovely Kevin at a disadvantage. It sticks in my throat that my barrister has to help someone who has made me feel cheated, bullied and vulnerable in court, and I have to pay for the privilege as does Joe Public because he is using up precious court time.

But to my horror the trial wasn't just about Dougall's law breaking, because he counterclaimed against me personally as part of the trial. He wanted damages (i.e. money) for breach of contract, breach of copyright and breach of confidentiality. He also claimed I made fraudulent statements about my financial situation. The court would not only need to consider his wrongdoing but would have to judge if I was personally guilty of the counter claims, which means I ended up in the witness box. And guess what? Despite the fact that he'd threatened me and my daughter blatantly and in writing; that he had attempted to liquidate my company without me owing him anything so that all my staff would lose their jobs; that he was a breath-taking liar, fraudster and crook; I had to stand for one and a half days and be interrogated by him face-to-face. How does this happen when he is up before court because of his behaviour? Why do I then have to defend myself before a judge to answer questions about my integrity and honesty?

As a woman, this man is allowed to stand over me in the witness box and use the personal information he gleaned to intimidatingly interrogate me in person. As he doesn't use a barrister he can pretty much ask what he wants because he's not professionally bound by a code of conduct and, as he did often, he can always rely on the excuse that he is naïve before court and they must give him some slack.

Needless to say, alongside the big fat imposing gait of Dougall, the judge was a man, as was my solicitor and the barrister. I was the only female in the room, save for the person with the lowly administrative task of writing the transcript, which I had to pay for. The stress and worry are unbelievable, because everyone in the courtroom knows that if you lose, you're finished, and if you win, he'll continue making your life hell for years afterwards by refusing to pay. It's worked for him before.

In his questioning, he decided to undermine and cast doubt on my personal integrity and trustworthiness. What this has to do with his own wrongdoing is hard to see. His 'cross examination' of me lasted one and a half days in the intimidating Royal Courts of Justice. He stated on oath, after swearing to tell the truth, the whole truth and nothing but the truth with his hand on a copy of the bible (because he's religious and his dad was a vicar), that:

- As he stipulated in court papers I **"set out to keep (my) former husband in the dark"** over financial dealings in my company.
- Knowingly evaded tax and national insurance payments because I don't actually have any employees. Wtf.
- Made fraudulent misrepresentation in relation to our finances and that my company was not in fact, solvent.
- Fabricated evidence and so did my solicitor.
- Was a liar (he said this many times).

- Had given false evidence (he has witnesses?!).
- Was, quote **"deranged and untrustworthy."**

All of these statements are plainly evidenced in his emails, his sworn witness statements and shown in court papers. The basis of these is unclear, and why they had anything to do with Dougall's own wrongdoing is not apparent. I wasn't allowed to draw attention to the fact that he used intimidating threats and had a long history of starting and winding up scores of companies so as not to pay his bills.

If you don't know how court appearances work (I didn't until that morning), you're not allowed to be coached on how to handle these type of questions, or how you should answer (despite what you see on television). Also, you're not allowed to talk to your solicitor or barrister about anything at all until the questioning has stopped. So overnight and in breaks you have no support and can't talk to anyone about what happened. You just sit there isolated on your own and in my case go home alone with no one to talk to, knowing that you have to go through it again the next day.

Should it be allowed that a man who has threatened a woman and her children can further intimidate her, asking personal questions that would never be asked of a man and have no bearing on the case in question? He was quite legitimately permitted to do this for a day and a half in front of other men, as part of the legal process. Our barrister said it was a good thing that all these personal attacks were being aimed at me because the judge would know that they were irrelevant and had no bearing on the case. It felt to me that the barrister couldn't care less how it made me feel and if the judge knew it was irrelevant why was it allowed?

Obviously (well looking back now it's obvious) we won in every respect. In essence, it was confirmed by the judge, given the evidence that he had passed himself off as my company, extracted money from clients using false invoices, stolen my brand, company documents and trademark and breached the contract we had signed between us. As to the counterclaims, the judge stated that allegations of fraud aimed at me were **"hopeless."** That's just about as damning as a judge can get. He then summed up by stating in conclusion, that **"every allegation of the counter-claim fails."** Phew!

My point is not that the law is an ass but that it favours those who know how to navigate it and are masters of filibuster. Business thieves, liars and cheats are free to leverage the system and draw out the pain for others so that it drags out for years and becomes so expensive that continued pursuit of justice is illogical and counterproductive.

When we eventually got the judgement, Dougall went to the Court of Appeal to explain the judge was incompetent, that my lawyer had fabricated evidence and that I had lied, amongst a litany of other injustices he felt he'd suffered. This adds yet more months to the process. Needless to say, every single point was turned down again but you are never sure that will be the outcome.

It's immensely stressful reading a new litany of lies and imagined events against you every time you think you get a little closer to a final resolution, because it exposes you to the prospect of the most magnificent financial loss on top of the non-payment you're owed. If you're a woman in business juggling family commitments, taking the lion's share of domestic responsibilities, naturally adverse to confrontation and lacking in confidence, then when you're pitched against an arrogant lying bully who'll use every weapon possible to undermine and discredit you, have you got the fight in you to take them on? Those types bet that you haven't and usually they get away with it. Of course, there are lots of men who just can't muster the energy to fight such people either, but I think women are far more likely to give up and vow never to run a business ever again.

Blistering vicious attack is a form of defence because it stops you from asking difficult and penetrating questions. The perpetrator can use them to distract from their own misdemeanours and the huge swathes of broken lives they have left behind them. They want everyone to know that they're an unwitting victim subject to outside malevolent forces that they cannot comprehend. Woe are they. I'm no psychiatrist or doctor, but it seems to me that those types believe they're the cleverest person in the room. Always.

There are a number of my friends that believe I was groomed by Dougall. They think he deliberately seeks out vulnerable or inexperienced individuals so that he can exploit them. He searches for people that are isolated and at such a low ebb that they're highly unlikely to be up for the fight. I didn't believe them at first, but now I think it's highly probable. A woman, going through a divorce after 29 years of marriage, living in rented accommodation with no personal effects except clothes, tired and anxious running a new business with fragile cashflow, responsible for paying staff each month weighing heavy and already waging a stressful court case where I'd been accused of signature fraud - I must've had 'vulnerable' seeping out of my pores.

The judge awarded costs at the rate of 95 percent against him. It's unusual for it to be this high, but it was clear that he had blatantly lied and gratuitously wasted court time, so the maximum costs were awarded. On paper this means that The Royal Courts of Justice in London legally obliged Dougall to personally pay £320,000 in legal and court costs (it had escalated that much). Note that I will not get a single penny. Not one. This amount is just to settle court fees and my solicitor and barrister which I had to pay as we went along. They loved it. The cut and thrust of the arguments, the drama and all along knowing they would get paid come what may.

If I want to get any money out of this horrific, draining episode for damages, I have to go to court with another action to sue him and it will all start again. Except of course, I can't do that now because he's been declared bankrupt. He owes over £2 million to HMRC alone and many more debts to banks, credit card companies and car leasing companies. He's disappeared now, last seen in Northern Ireland probably scamming more unsuspecting victims or pretending to be a business guru at an inflated hourly fee.

I did eventually get some of the money back to pay the barrister and lawyer although I ended up £80,000 out of pocket, but at least I got most of it. But what is important is that hopefully he has been damaged enough financially to seriously reconsider conning other businesspeople.

This is what business is like. It's exhausting, tough and stressful. It also diverts you from the main reason you started a company in the first place which is to proudly sell your services or products and to delight your customers. If you grow and become bigger you will face a court case or two along the way. You'll be bruised and downhearted a good few times.

Fundamentally, I think that some middle-aged middle-class

white men who have no scruples cannot accept that I run a business myself and that I'm good at it. Of course, I'm generalising, but most just don't seem able to believe it's possible. It doesn't align to anything they've ever known, seen and been told. Just like when I was growing up, the books, films and tv programmes that surrounded them didn't show women in business, ever.

Their mothers probably didn't work. Their wives would have fitted around their very important corporate jobs, as would their children. They don't have a sense of a woman being educationally or professionally capable, let alone equal and they're pretty certain you won't be up for a fight if it came to it. In my experience, mostly these types of men think that my business has been funded and set up by my husband, or I've inherited it, or I've been very lucky. Certainly Dougall couldn't fathom that I'd done it myself.

I can't help thinking though, that a guy in his 20s or 30s is likely to have seen his mum hold down a job. His partner is probably working too and she (if it is a she), would probably be comparably educated and experienced. Their frame of reference is different. Would they have chanced taking me to court thinking I would wilt before we got anywhere? I don't think they would.

The plain fact is, that in 2020, even if you take horrible people out of the equation, you still get bullied and harassed disproportionately. The gender pay gap is not just a myth but glaringly obvious. You do have to continue to suffer overt discrimination, unintentional discrimination, sexist comments, physical harassment and condescending 'advice'.

However, the upside, from my point of view, is that nobody wants to have sex with an old bird like me anymore or touch me up – that's probably because I'm 60 now and the ideal woman age for men, as we now know, is 22.

CHAPTER 11
Losing my water wings

**"Why can't a woman
be more like a man?"**

Henry Higgins

Then I got to think that maybe all this has happened to me because I'm doing something wrong. None of my friends have a weird eventful life like me. Well, who does? Am I culpable? Is it the way I present myself and the way I do things that inadvertently encourage discrimination or invite bullies? Is it partly my fault? I started asking myself this and wondered if other women thought this too.

My absolute belief for so long, was that the path of least resistance, the one to aid your career progression, the one that would make you liked by both men and women and protect your children, was to flatter inadequate, aggressive men. Intelligent, secure men don't want, or need, to be flattered. Women so often act as the 'glue' in professional and social situations. This works not just socially but also professionally - turn your head to the side, look like you're interested when they're very dull and praise their professional ability, even though often, they're much less experienced or not as good at their job as you. When they offer you advice, although they've little idea what they're talking about, smile and pretend you're listening.

I'm good at that but I'm not proud of it. I learnt to do it just right, so it isn't too obvious and it's utterly convincing. I still do it, 35 bloody years on. It's no coincidence that I'd been doing it in my marriage to make sure the complicated structures that bind partners, their children and their wider families together, remained in harmony. It was a great training ground. I perfected it. But now I'm not inside an organisational structure, I'm at the head of a business I own, so I can create the rules and the culture.

After reading *Postfeminism and Organisation* by a friend of mine, Dr. Patricia Lewis, I think I had a well-respected and successful corporate career because I carefully calibrated my gender and sexuality, simultaneously embracing masculinity and femininity. I will only do masculinity in combination with feminine behaviours and practices, so that women will like me too. I got good at doing masculinity despite being female, but I made sure that I was never too far up one end of that continuum. I can't shed my gender, nor my class but I've worked very hard to appear both asexual and classless when at work. This meant that as I rose in power and influence, I was seen as less threatening and obviously this minimised confrontation. I've had to lose a huge chunk of my femininity to succeed at work. Being fiercely intelligent and working extremely hard is not enough. The saying 'be so good they can't ignore you' is sadly untrue if you're female.

The traditional feminine norm of non-confrontation is my natural default position. Consistently surrounded by dominant masculine regimes, feminism and femininity didn't seem compatible. To succeed it was obvious you had to mask your rivalry with men and find a work-compatible gender identity that was neither male or female. I know this has seriously messed with my head though and it's so utterly exhausting.

I didn't entirely change these previous attitudes and behaviours even though I now had my own company and no career, husband or dependent children to worry about. In my private sector SME world, if you don't network and go to male-orientated business events and dinners, you don't get work. It's not the same in every sector, but it is in most. I'm responsible for new business development. CEOs generally are, they have to be, as the face of the business. And it's relentless. My staff would be out of a job if I didn't endure these awful business events. Those men may not always know how to run a small business from scratch, but they're still very well connected, and they've mostly created the rules of the environment you find yourself in. You need them, whether you like it or not.

I now understand Germaine Greer's quote from what seems like a hundred years ago. She said: **"I'm sick of pretending that some fatuous male's self-important pronouncements are the objects of my undivided attention."** Yep. I thought you were a pain in the arse and a very difficult woman all those years ago, but I know what you mean now, and by the way I know where Dame Helen Mirren was coming from now, too.

I think my problem is that if you're very good at subtle flattery, sparkling humorous conversation and creating harmony and you're female, you will attract men who want to 'try'. Lots of them. Therefore, although I'm not the prettiest woman in the world by any means, and I'm definitely not 22 anymore, my ability at being the glue and/ or the person who is perceived as being utterly fascinated by dull overly confident older men, is that you're going to suffer the most inappropriate sexual advances and behaviour. They go hand in hand.

I've only recently realised that's how it works because I think I was just doing it intuitively to survive and thrive. Most especially, if you're lacking in confidence and brought up to be polite and not embarrass somebody publicly. In turn those bullies are outstanding at spotting that type of vulnerability. I don't dress provocatively, never have. No plunging neck lines, slit skirts or bare shoulders, because that's not me – it's just never been my style. But if I had, it may have protected me. It might've shown how confident I am, and that if you mess with me I'm going to call you out and possibly publicly.

If you haven't suffered awful sexual harassment, is it because you're not attractive and it doesn't exist? No, it's because those 'tryers' have sussed out that you will possibly out them and very loudly. Would they approach Karren Brady for example, who has famously said she has encountered sexism in her career but never sexual harassment even though she's spent most of her professional life working in English football? As Villanelle from *Killing Eve* chillingly said in one episode: **"You should really ask before you touch a person."** Well, with Villanelle you would ask first, or not at all because the consequences are too scary.

Karren Brady has never encountered sexual harassment

Karren had rich parents, she must have because they could afford two r's in her first name. She was very well educated and I'm assuming, self-assured enough to tell them to piss off and very loudly or worse. Better off homing in on someone who won't embarrass you and will not only engage with you but look interested. Ironically, I think those lovely ladies who are confident or wear amazing clothes and look sexy unlike me, might actually be giving signals that they're going to give you a tough ride if you approach them. A complicated theory and possibly wrong but interesting nonetheless.

I think the approach I've taken will attract much criticism and seem utterly ridiculous and my own fault. On reflection, not on purpose you understand, I accidentally crafted my techniques to make sure I stayed in a monogamous, on my part, 32-year relationship, bring up two balanced children and be successful in business completely on my own. The result of my attempt at domestic survival and business success, has inadvertently encouraged sexual harassment and abuse to rain down on me. I'm sure I'm not alone in making this mistake.

You can say what you like about the #metoo campaign, but so many women like me know exactly what it means. I'm bored of it. Weary of it. Depressed that it doesn't seem to be getting that much better. I'm particularly exasperated by men (and sometimes women) that harass those brave enough to make such statements as I'm making. I know I will receive the cruellest abuse on social media for writing down what's happened to me and what I think about it.

The treatment that people like the outrageously clever Dame Mary Beard, Professor of Classics at Newnham College, Cambridge, have suffered online is scandalous. There's overwhelming evidence that women and members

Mary Beard suffers constant sexist abuse on social media

of ethnic minority groups are disproportionately targeted on social media platforms like Twitter, and the vast share of the threats are carried out by men. The constant barrage of verbal attacks includes death threats and explicitly described vile sexual abuse. When a female journalist dared to suggest that it might be nice to keep Jane Austen on our £10 bank notes rather than replace her with a man, she was repeatedly threatened with rape and decapitation. One perpetrator was arrested but many others taunted police online and stepped up their activity in defiance.

In her book *Women and Power,* Mary Beard examines the threats women have received online. She states:

"It doesn't much matter what line you take as a woman, if you venture into traditional male territory, the abuse comes anyway. It is not what you say that prompts it, it's simply the fact that you're saying it. And that matches the details of the threats themselves. They include a fairly predictable menu of rape, bombing, murder and so forth . . . But a significant subsection is directing at silencing the woman."

She explains the advice you are given (mostly by men obviously) is not to rise to the perpetrators or to answer them, less you give them the attention they possibly crave but as she points out: **"It risks leaving the bullies in unchallenged occupation of the playground."** She goes on to say that the abusers want you to be silenced as a woman, and the advice you are given ironically gives them exactly what they want.

Julia Gillard the former Australian Prime Minister was previously a high-flying partner in a law firm. Although fiercely clever and experienced, none of that prepared her for the vehement abuse she suffered during her time in office, not just as a woman but as a woman without children at that. A senior opposition politician publicly described her as **"deliberately barren"**, the leader of one of Australia's biggest companies called her **"a non-productive old cow"** and a radio interviewer brazenly asked her on air if her husband was gay. This was aside from the 'ditch the witch' campaign to try to oust her out of office. All of which are just some of the more printable insults. It's hard to come up with any equivalent male-orientated derogatory comments because men created the language and environment, so there just aren't any.

As I've got older I've come to be incensed about it. It's another way to ensure that women become too scared to voice their opinions. It's not worth it and I'm not worth it we all reason, contrary to the l'Oreal maxim. Women have to pay a very high price if they want to be heard. Surely sticking your head above the parapet as a Jeffrey Epstein, Harvey Weinstein or Donald Trump victim is the most ridiculously brave or stupid thing ever. As Emma Thompson put it during an interview on *Newsnight* in her description of what she called a system of harassment, belittling, bullying, interference and pestering: **"We can't keep making the women to whom this happens responsible."** Well, bollocks. I now feel brave enough to talk because this is my last working gig. I don't need a cv or references anymore and frankly I've got to the age where finally as I start my seventh decade, I just don't care what people think about me.

I left my husband in 2016 and a year later in June 2017 we were divorced, almost 30 years from our wedding day. I had stopped all contact with him by then, because he had deliberately maxed out our credit cards and run up our first ever overdraft (to the tune of £14,000) before separate finances could be arranged. His emails, texts and phone calls were hugely abusive and I felt terrorised. It was personal anger and social embarrassment at being left, of course. I chose not to reveal the details of the abuse to my children or that I was frightened at what he might do. He was leaning on them a lot, tugging at their heart strings to get their support through lonely and grief-stricken days. So, because of my guilt I suppose I wanted them to carry on doing that and not put them off propping him up. I thought that was what your friends were for, not your children. Needless to say though, he met someone else very soon afterwards.

As befits a good cliché, this person was a 'friend' of mine, who mysteriously visited him two weeks after I walked out, even though she hadn't apparently been to our house for a good few years. I don't know she had my husband's number. They gradually started seeing each other and he unthinkingly brought her to our daughter's wedding as his partner before the divorce was finalised. I obviously was on my own but I could see that he wasn't very well at all. He didn't join in as the life and soul of the party as usual. As someone who knew him better than anyone else in the world, including himself, there was definitely something wrong.

Despite my personal situation, the court cases and the relentless uphill battle against misogyny, the company began to stabilise and grow. We were getting continuous new business, retaining our clients and growing in profits. But a month after the divorce came through in June 2017, my now ex-husband, was diagnosed with cancer and became very ill. You can, or possibly cannot, imagine the guilt I felt. Was it because I'd left him? Was it because his diet of lots of red meat and hard drinking had finally caught up with him? Or both? Or just plain bad luck?

He started living with his new girlfriend who is ironically a vegan. But she didn't seem to be very good at looking after him or cooking for him through his illness. My daughter made protein boosting meals and drove from London (some 70 miles) to put them in his freezer to ensure he was getting as much balanced nutritious food as possible. Both daughters took turns in taking him to his chemo sessions when his girlfriend was, for some reason, unavailable. She also went on holiday with a friend leaving him behind for a couple of weeks at a critical point in his treatment, which seemed inexplicable to me. He became more and more ill and was in a permanent hospital bed after his treatment was clearly not working. He'd married his new partner by then, knowing that he would be dead very soon because he wanted to leave his money and pensions to her, which is fair enough.

Our daughters were amazing, visiting him all the time and eventually sleeping next to him in his hospital room, sharing stories, playing games and videos from their child-hood, even if they weren't sure he could hear. They came back to my rented accommodation for a quick shower or a proper home cooked meal every couple of days. I stayed away. It didn't seem right to cut across his new life even though I had literally spent the whole of my adulthood with him and we had two children together. He had always supported my career and helped me go for jobs which I might not have had the confidence to do if it wasn't for him, but I had chosen to leave him and I was not part of his life now.

Then at midnight one night when I couldn't sleep, I got in the car and drove the 20 minutes to hospital. I don't know why I was so compelled to go and I went into his room, his wife was nowhere to be seen and the girls left me alone with him. He could barely see or speak. He looked 100 years old. You might think that standing there I would be really compelled to stab him. But I didn't. I told him I loved him which was true. Love being a very complicated thing and not something where you get to choose how you feel. The only words he could say were: **"I thought I would never see you again"** before he drifted back into unconsciousness and I took the car back home leaving our daughters to maintain their usual routine. I never saw him again.

A few days later on 8 October 2018, ten weeks after he had got remarried, my eldest daughter rang to tell me that he had definitely stopped breathing and that they were going to find a doctor and was it OK to invoke the 'do not resuscitate' thing. I thought it was unlikely that anything would help now. At the last it was the three of them together. This troubled, funny, loving, violent, abusive man let go of his life and on a Monday afternoon in October sitting in my office, I put down my phone and realised I was finally totally released and free.

Over the next few days the girls stayed with me and we planned the funeral because his wife said she was too upset to do it. They worked out what they wanted to say as a eulogy. It was beautiful – funny and sad, as the best ones always are. We played the songs he liked at full volume, deciding which ones to use and we recounted all his much-loved jokes for the order of service which we designed and printed. We laughed and we cried. He wanted to be buried in a cardboard coffin. It looked horribly dull, so we convinced the funeral parlour to let us line one of their family rooms with plastic sheeting and then spent an hour splattering it with paint, so it looked like his favourite Jackson Pollock painting.

To fulfil his wishes, I then spent the weirdest night of my life washing my dead ex-husband's famous barbecue shirt and shorts which I had bought him years before. I put in loads of fabric softener so it smelt really nice. I then ironed them beautifully and hung them on a hanger so he could wear them stretched out in his paint splattered cardboard coffin as requested. His favourite shoes were a bit old and stinky though, so I decided to put them in the recycling bin. No one would know. I can't remember what I did about the socks. After the funeral the girls went home, no longer living on hold and back to their normal lives at last.

So you see, I can now say it like it is. Nobody can hurt me more than I've already been hurt and that does bestow a type of power and the need to tell the truth. It also somehow freed me to completely devote everything to the business. A new chapter begins. I felt cleansed and allowed to c oncentrate on me. It was deeply sad, but it was also scary and exciting.

CHAPTER 12
Not waving but drowning

"There is no greater agony
than carrying an untold story
inside you. Weighed down and
exhausted by the effort of
hiding your unhappiness."

Maya Angelou

I can say quite loudly now, that there's still rampant sexism, some is on purpose and some accidental. It might be a bit better but it's everywhere. This is not a post-feminist world at all. That's a false dawn, particularly in business. Middle aged men didn't used to know their behaviour was appalling, but now surely, they must do and the good(ish) guys are looking back and realising that it was wrong. Some even understand that they've had a terrible personal effect on some of the women they've harassed in the past.

Increasingly, not least because it's affecting the bottom-line and the gender pay gap is way too visible, there's genuine male recognition that we have a problem that's not going to go away and it's gaining momentum. But the guys in power don't know how to fix it. No wonder, because it's complicated and they don't have enough women around them to work through it. In 2015, software engineer Kate Heddleston explained what she thought was happening, with particular reference to the tech industry:

"Women ... are the canary in the coal mine. Normally when the canary in the coal mine starts dying you know the environment is toxic and you should get the hell out. Instead, ... industry is looking at the canary, wondering why it can't breathe, saying 'Lean in, canary. Lean in!' When one canary dies they get a new one because getting more canaries is how you fix the lack of canaries, right? Except the problem is that there isn't enough oxygen in the coal mine, not that there are too few canaries."

If you want to see an example of this just look at British politics. Women are actively encouraged to enter parliament at every election but that barely stems the flow of the numbers who leave as quickly as they can. Michelle Obama has constantly been asked if she would ever enter politics, her reply as stated in her memoir *Becoming* was: **"I've never been a fan of politics, and my experience over the last ten years has done little to change   that . . . I continue to be put off by the nastiness."** There are lots of excuses used to explain why women leave so quickly, but each time it's the symptoms which are examined and not the cause. It's the whole environment and culture that needs changing but instead they just put more effort into finding new canaries. As Mary Beard put it **"you can't easily fit women into a structure that is already coded as male; you have to change the structure."**

Another example was revealed by a very talented and clever female friend of mine who recently went for a job interview as a CEO for a charity. She has a PhD, solid experience and a cool, calm but determined and steely manner. She was encouraged that there were more women on the shortlist for the job than men. But in her interview, they said she was too softly spoken, and as they had two very aggressive and macho old-fashioned men on the trustee board that needed shouting down, they therefore couldn't appoint her. It didn't strike them at all, that the culture should change or even that it could. They were going to adopt the tactic of shouting louder and being more aggressive than the culprits, thus perpetuating it. None of the women candidates got the job, which could just be a coincidence of course.

In her 'canary' observation, Heddleston's reference is to Sheryl Sandberg's book *Lean In*. Personally, I find what Sandberg's written, hard to swallow. First, because I don't think Meta is a truly ethical company and she was in a very influential position when it was clear they were misusing personal data. She's not exactly my ideal female business role model. Secondly, advice on insisting your partner does more parenting and their fair share of housework is a dream for many women. They're just not living in the type of household where that conversation can take place, if indeed, they do have partners and are not trying to get through as a single parent. The contention that possibly trading sex as a reward in this scenario is not helpful either.

Sheryl Sandberg: "Beware the cute bucket"

Thirdly, Sandberg's use of terminology is frustrating and annoying, but that may be because I'm not American. Her warning, even if it has a degree of truth, that if you're too nice at work you run the risk of being put into the 'cute bucket', makes me want to vomit into said bucket. Some of the book is truly valuable, but most of it I find highly amusing because the lens on which her perspective is based is a little suspect when you consider she's worth $1.9 billion. Yes, billion, not million. You can get a lot of domestic help with that amount of dosh.

Despite the fact that I agree women should try and over-come their lack of confidence and willingness to challenge aggression and bias, I'm still depressed about the current situation. #metoo and #timesup have become so public that the more intransigent males have used this to position themselves as victims. In their eyes, women are now unfairly targeting men when there isn't really a problem anymore.

Recently, some guys in science, technology, engineering and mathematics came out strongly to say they're the victim of 'reverse discrimination'.

This was revealed in a study of men in the sector by Pew Research. It showed that 19 percent have experienced gender discrimination and believe they can't get a fair break in the industry and 7 percent think their gender makes it harder for them to succeed at work. Is that all? 19 percent and 7 percent? What that means to me is that 93 percent don't think their gender makes it harder to succeed. Doh.

"Today the white male is the enemy," said one chap from Intel who participated in the research but sort of forgot that the 'oppressed' group to which he belongs occupy 77.8 percent of his employer's engineering roles and

80.2 percent of its executive jobs. Stuart Rose's comments echo in my head again: **"There really are no glass ceilings despite the fact that some of you moan about it all the time... I mean what else do you want for God's sake?"** Many men like them genuinely can't see it. They don't notice as they're too wrapped up in themselves, don't really care or it's a deliberate act. Is it generational? God, I hope so.

Even so, The Institute for Fiscal Studies and UCL interviewed 3,500 families during the covid lockdown and found that mums, on average, were doing more childcare and more housework than dads who have the same work arrangements. They are the ones planning meals, creating timetables and downloading learning resources for children - along with dozens of other domestic tasks such as cleaning, washing, food shopping and cooking. In total mothers who were working from home were able to do only one hour of uninterrupted work for every three hours done by fathers.

The only households where both sets of parents were sharing childcare and housework equally are those in which the mum is still getting paid work but the dad had stopped working. One of their researchers reported: **"However, mothers in these households are doing paid work during an average of five hours a day, in addition to doing the same amount of domestic work as their partner, who is not working."**

Comments from other similar research include: **"I'm the main wage earner and yet I also seem to be the one who stops work to make lunch and dinner."** And: **"[My partner] is furloughed and yet my work telephone calls are interrupted by the children asking questions, while daddy is just watching**

Netflix." The Institute for Fiscal Studies has also reported that mothers are almost 50 percent more likely than fathers to have lost their jobs during the pandemic. They warn that this will cause **"lasting harm"** to women's careers as the result of lockdown.

Tessa West, the author of a recent book called *Jerks at Work*, is a professor of social psychology at New York University. She argues that after covid and working from home, so many people are dreading going back to their workplaces. She describes seven types of 'jerks' including 'kiss up/kick downers' that have a single goal in mind, which is to climb to the top by any means necessary. 'Credit stealers' who seem like friends but will betray your trust if your idea is good enough to steal and 'Bulldozers' who are seasoned and well-connected. They're not afraid to flex their muscles to get what they want by taking over group discussions and rendering their colleagues powerless to stop them, through fear and intimidation.

She adds that there's a lot of research on how social class affects behaviour. She claims that poorer people are nicer because they haven't been tutored in the secret Machiavellian code by white-collar parents who have experience of such things. They're more communal and want to work on teams where there's equality, except so often they can't find it. She claims: **"They get taken advantage of and not invited to things (and) they are more likely to get excluded."** Her conclusion is that nicer people (of all classes, genders and backgrounds) are attracted to flatter hierarchies as they instinctively know this is not where the big sharks swim.

She is currently conducting a study in London on senior

surgeons: "**One career where we see a lot of jerks is in surgery. Senior surgeons tend to be pretty arrogant. There is a strong hierarchy . . . and where you see those rigid hierarchies you see this behaviour.**" Consequently, she says there is a real reluctance among kinder, nicer people to return to the workplace environment after covid-imposed working from home. They've enjoyed avoiding the jerks who have found it more difficult to throw their weight around via remote working.

Her advice to employers is that such people show themselves very early on and pretending their technical ability is more important than interpersonal skills is a mistake: "**That can be very costly. The company loses other employees.**"

Yes, the good ones who silently disagree and will just move companies in protest but not tell you about their reasoning. Will it ever become more equal?

CHAPTER 13
Lifeguards to the rescue

"Sexism is a man screaming he has a better temperament than a woman who's been patiently waiting to speak after being interrupted ten times."

Nick Prayner

There is still violence and discrimination against women across the globe, and girls in particular are undergoing the most appalling abuse every day according to United Nations and ActionAid:

- 120 million girls globally have experienced forced sex or other sexual acts.
- 99 percent of Egyptian women have been sexually harassed.
- 84 percent of Brazilian women reported being sexually harassed by the police.
- 90 percent of women and girls in Papua New Guinea have experienced some form of violence on public transport.

'Women Against Sexual Harassment', Rome

The huge survey across the 28 member states by the European Union Agency for Fundamental Rights found 44 percent of women in the UK have experienced physical or sexual violence, not harassment or name calling actual violence. The highest is in Denmark (52 percent) and the lowest in Germany (35 percent). This can't be described as post-feminism in any context . . .

Then in March 2021 Sarah Everard was kidnapped in South London where I was brought up. Metropolitan police officer, Wayne Couzens falsely arrested her under the pretence that she had breached covid regulations and drove her to a place in Kent where he raped and strangled her, before burning her body and disposing of her remains in a nearby pond.

Thousands of women went online to share tales of intimidating prowlers, proclaiming how lucky they were to escape Sarah's dreadful fate. There was an outpouring of grief and anger which revealed the appalling misogyny affecting women's lives. It's not just me, it's everywhere, is what became very clear. The singer and songwriter Nadine Shah said she had been followed home **"too many times to count."** In one incident, she wrote: **"I could hear them plotting explicitly what they were going to do to me and laughing."** Diane Abbott, the Labour MP for Hackney North, said that years of navigating harassment and violence meant she crossed streets automatically if she heard footsteps behind her: **"It is the habit of a lifetime to try and keep safe."** Kate McCann, a political correspondent at *Sky News*, described the lengths women routinely go to stay safe on journeys home:

"We take the longer, better-lit route, push the fear aside for the voice that says 'Don't be daft, you've every right to walk home alone at night and be safe'. Keys gripped between fingers we map the corner shops we could duck into en route. Swap shoes for trainers in case we need to run. Keep our music low or turned off. One eye is always on the person in front or behind — would they help me, might they be a threat? Should I cross the road, would that make it worse?"

"At 14 I was assaulted in the street, in my school uniform, at 8.15 in the morning," Polly Mackenzie, Chief Executive of the think tank Demos, said, I was **"pushed into a hedge and groped."** Dr Julia Patterson, Chief Executive of the group Every Doctor, recalled that she was attacked in the street by a man while she was in medical school, and suffered injuries so severe she had to go to A&E. When she went to the police, an officer made advances to her and then, when she declined them, sent her belongings and evidence to another station. **"I didn't report him because I felt stupid, like I'd done something wrong . . . Sarah could be any one of us and I'm devastated for her."**

Nathalie Emmanuel, who has appeared in *Game of Thrones*, said she was only 10 or 11 the first time she was flashed by a man, and it had happened repeatedly. She also described being followed by men, in cars or on foot, and groped by strangers:

"When I was like 21, two young teenage boys put their hands up my skirt. The predatory behaviour of men is devastating women and it's something that is learnt young. Women can't keep screaming

about it . . . there has to come a point where men check themselves and other men and boys for their behaviour. We are tired."

Depressingly, that sums it up. We are tired of putting up with it.

The Centre for Women's Justice said the outpouring of stories revealed the level of fear women had to deal with, adding: **"That fear is based on a victim-blaming misogynistic culture and a woefully inadequate criminal justice system which provides near-impunity for rapists and alarming failures in tackling domestic abuse."** Yes, it's a fact that there are teeny weeny conviction rates for rape and sexual assault.

It seems that when they come up in court, because unimaginably brave women push for it, the victim wish they hadn't bothered. At Thameside Court in March 2021, Javid Miah from Oldham was let off a prison sentence after he followed a young woman, wrestled her to the ground and sexually assaulted her. She only escaped because she managed to press the SOS function to call the police on her phone during the attack. The prosecutor who should be making a strong case to protect her was Peter Conroy. Miah's lawyer Saul Comish said in mitigation: **"This offence was quite opportunistic"** and therefore he has a **"low risk of re-offending."**

He persuaded the judge that he should escape jail because he would **"lose his job."** David Quarnby JP decided the sentence. Any thoughts on the line up in court and how this poor young woman must have felt surrounded by all these men? Perhaps there could have been a female judge, but there again in England and Wales, of 106 High Court judges, only 22 are women and in the Court of Appeal, eight of 39 judges are female. Not enough to go around.

Seeing as the prosecutor, defence lawyer and judge allowed Miah to walk free, the victim told police: **"Since the assault . . . I do not know if he knows my route to work. I am scared to walk anywhere. I will have to rely on my friends or family to drive me to work out of fear."** She effectively went through her ordeal twice and now she is the prisoner.

I thought that things would change much more dramatically for my daughters than it has. Now they both have their own children and, as I hoped, I am a doting and extremely proud grandmother. Perhaps my grandchildren will grow up and things will have changed so much that they will laugh about the fact that there used to be a work bias against women. They'll all be paid the same and can carry out their job without being sexually harassed and won't believe our stories and think we're exaggerating. They'll have heard of a plethora of amazing historical women achievers and be used to successful women commenting on the economy and the world of business. They'll know exactly who Stephanie Shirley is but won't know anything about Stuart Rose. To them that old world will be as quaint and as distant as telex machines and having an outside toilet.

With my working life nearing its end, I have two observations about the future. One is a real cause for concern and the other gives me great optimism . . . .

Almost every business in the future will be a digital tech business. Retail, healthcare, education, leisure, manufacturing, all are being shaped, yes by our response to the covid outbreak but also by the amazing advances in technology, artificial intelligence and robotics. You could be a florist, food producer, software engineer, accountant, doctor, teacher or personal trainer. It doesn't matter, your world can't survive without technology. It's moving rapidly and visibly changing our high streets, workplaces and communities.

There are moves by our new generation of brilliant techie men to 'pinkify' our apps, games, household products, systems and infrastructures. They recognise that women generally control purchasing decisions, and so they genuinely want to make it more inclusive. They're trying to second guess what add-ons and specific functionality might make technology more amenable and relevant to women. But it's not the same as designing things for us from the ground up.

Healthtech and edtech in particular are often failing to solve, or even spot, female needs, and as we know, women founders are not getting funded to anywhere near the same level to do this for themselves even when there are markets ripe for their ideas.

Only 17 percent of people in the tech sector are women and as we know, the key players overwhelming employ men at a leadership level. This new world is literally being shaped from a male perspective again. It's so frightening. We must get our daughters into tech and digital and now, or a new world order will be created that marginalises women all over again. They don't have to be programmers or coders but their entry into tech has to be facilitated, or structures modified to make this possible so there's an equitable input. We need to work out why our young women achieve 50 percent parity at school level in science, engineering and technology quite willingly, but then there is an alarming drop off. By the time it gets to university graduation and the job market they bale out. Those subjects are attractive at an academic level, but even though they're good at it, they're put off at the professional level.

In my job I work with a lot of start-ups and accelerators. Women seem particularly attracted to the food sector, health, beauty and the arts. Many are in micro-businesses or have become freelance so as to work around childcare responsibilities or to allow homeworking. And yet there is a huge shortage of tech skills. According to Tech London Advocates we need to fill another 650,000 tech jobs in London alone in the next five years. I would urge our new generation of young women to stop aspiring to make chutney or being an interior designer and get into digital. We need you. We really do. You don't have to be a coder, it could be project management, design, analysis, all sorts of interesting areas around the tech space.

However, despite the lack of women going into tech, I'm optimistic because men in their 20s and 30s have watched their mums and sisters hold down important and good jobs. They mostly have more respect for women and recognise that diversity is a positive and stimulating thing. Surely, we will work out how to overcome this, because with this generation, in general, there is a consensus that having women and an ethnically diverse workforce is essential and needed now.

I thoroughly believe in this generation. Born in the 1990s and afterwards, I'm encouraged by the fact that they're untainted by growing up in the appalling pervasive sexist culture of the 1970s. Both males and females are inspiring. Thankfully, they haven't read Leviticus. I find in general that they're considerate, worried about the planet and they couldn't care less if someone is black, white, gay, straight, Muslim, Christian, male or female, if indeed they notice at all.

They want things to be better all-around and for everyone. I adore and admire them. They're slowly replacing the likes of the lovely Kevin and Philip Green and all those, who in my opinion, still don't get it and probably believe that Jimmy Savile, Max Clifford, Harvey Weinstein, Rolf Harris, Donald Trump et al, were just unlucky because they're victims of opportunistic women leveraging the #metoo movement to extract money or personal publicity.

The attractive Harvey Weinstein at the height of his powers

Sir Jimmy Savile OBE, probably Britain's most prolific predatory sex offender, allowed to operate apparently 'undetected' until after his death

Donald Trump, 45th President of the United States and a vulnerable, self-proclaimed victim of opportunistic women.

My observation then, is that it's still difficult for women to call it out, for all sorts of highly complex reasons, much of it down to women's intrinsic lack of confidence and a primal need to be the glue that holds things together. Yes, we need to get over it, and move forward, but it's still hard. The discrimination we've endured silently and in isolation, has largely been a personal one, it's never been construed by most of us as a political or group problem, until now.

But the thing that I'm most enthused by, is men calling it out. I've just started to see this generation be vocal about the most dreadful injustice that's been going on. They're not impressed that society has allowed it to happen unchallenged until very recently. They generally haven't risen to the highest powers yet, that's still the preserve of much older white men, but they will do.

Convicted paedophile Rolf Harris CBE leaving court. The judge said: *"You have shown no remorse for your crimes at all."* He spent three years in jail for 12 indecent assaults on four girls including an eight year old and his daughter's friend.

Caitlin Moran wrote in 2021: **"Police have advised women not to go out on their own after dark." How long for? For… ever. We're just presuming it will go on like this… for ever. It's a silent, unwritten law for women."** She then suggested on Twitter that there should be a legally enforceable curfew for men after dark. Obviously, there was a huge amount of outrage from men saying it was unfair to be punished when they had done nothing wrong. Of course, there are many, many men who are appalled at violence aimed at women. Something they would never ever dream of doing themselves even in the worst of circumstances. Her response was that:

"Currently, women have to stay at home – but women have done nothing wrong. It is unfair for women. . . . After all, the worst thing about a legal curfew for men is that, if you break it, you would be arrested. The worst thing that happens to women . . . is: they die."

A male curfew is never going to happen and I'm not sure I would want it to, although it would be nice if it was law for one day a week. Think of it! But Caitlin's message was that:

"Women alone can't stop men raping, hurting, scaring and killing other women. We need men, these good men, to help us . . . Tell your 'creepy', 'odd' mate his behaviour is unacceptable. Discuss it within your male friendship group. Saying, "That's not cool, dude," the first time someone catcalls, may well mean it's also the *last* time he catcalls. Whole lifetimes of behaviours only grow when they're tolerated, or shrugged off, or laughed over. Men grow up in a climate of other men. You can change that climate."

Yes, yes, yes. To repeat Nathalie Emmanuel again: **"Women can't keep screaming about it . . . there has to come a point where men check themselves and other men and boys for their behaviour."**

I also believe women need help and these 'good' men can really come to our assistance, and I would be very grateful if they could. It's not women that are incapable, there just aren't enough of us at the top level to turn the tide. This is a whole world problem; apolitical, cross-generational, genderless, classless and not about race, religion or colour either. If we can get past all the media outrage, the vitriolic abuse and counter arguments, something very special could happen, to the benefit of everyone.

If men can refuse to speak at a conference when there's not a gender or race balance, it's uncomfortable for the organisers. If a man can interfere when they see an act of misogyny or male bias, it'll have more effect. I'm sorry but it will. If there's an event where it's ok to leer and touch women, they can complain and leave. They can isolate and make these misogynistic bullies into social pariahs, politely but firmly. This shows the landscape is no longer dictated or owned by the sexists and the sexual harassers – they're now in a foreign land, not us. Then the tectonic plates of the old language, rules and social rituals might just shift irreversibly.

I don't want to be seen as a victim because I'm not and I don't want to be seen as too old and cynical to take this on myself; I'm going to try harder to do that. But if you're a man and you think this all has to change too, I implore you to help me (and us) accelerate the demise of the old-world order, because frankly it's taking too bloody long for women to do it on their own.

And what of my dreams and attempt at emulating the final destination of Hannah Snell and the other badass historical women I've described? Did my business experiment, persistence and hard work pay off despite some very wobbly moments? I said that I wanted to get to a point where I proved I could run a successful business by uniting profit with purpose and then hopefully sell it to realise the initial investment. I wanted to get enough money for my own modest but comfortable pension and buy myself a house instead of renting. I was hoping I might have grandchildren by then and, you never know, meet some nice new chap and settle down into a relatively boring and uneventful life.

As you know the grandchildren dream has come true although it's very sad that my husband never got to meet them. He obviously didn't deserve that despite everything, but they make me so happy and I've let go of the guilt that I have them all to myself without him being a part of their life.

And notwithstanding the best attempts of late payers, downturns in the economy, crises of confidence, covid, crying quietly in the dark, career mistakes and some wrong turns, the company with just 20 or so wonderful people ended up with a very profitable £2.5 million turnover in our fifth year. We won numerous awards too, but I am most proud of our 'employer' accolades which recognised our CSR commitments and flexible, family-friendly working practices and those 'no qualifications needed' recruitment policies. It seems that you actually can be a corporate citizen and ethical employer and achieve a net (not gross) profit of 40 percent.

In the process we managed to get over £60 million in cash or tax benefits through to small business owners, helping them grow and create new jobs. We also sponsored local clubs and charities as much as we could. See how wonderful cleaners, snipers, penguin experts, dental receptionists and car salesmen can be? That is, when you let them have the freedom to shine.

What I've learnt is that high performing teams are those that are more diverse in every sense, rather than more academically intelligent. I've learnt that great businesses unite profit and purpose. They have a point of view with a strong backbone because when you don't know what you believe or what the company believes in, everything becomes an argument. Everything is debateable. When you stand for something, decisions become obvious. There's almost no debate because the answer is clear to everyone.

I've also learnt that to be a good leader is about how you react to stress. Conveying cool, calm authority, without a trace of fear, even when the shit is hitting the fan literally everywhere or you are at your very lowest ebb. That's the moment everyone looks to you to know what to do and how they should react. It's when people decide whether to follow you or not - right then and in the future. A cool decisive head and incisive decision-making is needed. I hope that I have achieved the Lao Tzu maxim which is: **"When the best leader's work is done the people say we did it ourselves."**

Our monumental success attracted a lot of interest from potential buyers during 2019. Both Brady and me, have been consistently laughed at by some of the regional accountancy firms who were appalled that unqualified people could offer a specific type of financial service to small businesses. They tried to undermine us. They made up stories that we were shysters and chancers muscling in on traditional accountant territory, but we never rose to the bait, just smiled wearily and carried on. We called them the rhinoceroses because they were thick skinned, short sighted and charged a lot. We were always way better at customer service, but such snide remakes just spurred us on to be better at the technical aspects than any of our competitors.

There are too few organisations that really understand customer service at the highest level, and too many examples of getting it wrong. Take the late lamented British motorbike industry. The key marques rested on past reputation and kept their heads down designing and producing motorbikes, using the equipment, skills and technology they had always done. The only problem was they forgot to look up and ask the British public what they wanted, as trends gradually changed. Unfortunately for them Kawasaki, Honda and Suzuki had – ironic how British kamikaze tactics failed to beat Japanese companies in the war for sales.

Some restaurants produce orgasmic food. They employ the best chefs, they spend thousands on doing the place up, pay celebrities to eat there and spend a fortune on the laundry bill. But eating lobster with truffled chicken quenelles is just not enough. All the money goes on the glitz and the service is an afterthought. When you arrive you wait 15 minutes before being asked what you'd like to drink. You can't have a starter from one menu and a main course from another and there's no toilet roll in the ladies. And obviously when you ask what the soup of the day is, the waitress hasn't a clue. But call centres, not restaurants, are the ones that take the amoretti biscuit. I hate them with a vengeance. They go against everything I've ever been taught about putting the customer first. The whole set up is for their convenience not ours. Who on earth dreamed up the concept of talking to an automated robot voice, where you have to stop listening to look at your phone to find the 'star' button, and when you get it back to your earhole you missed the last instruction?

Who thought it would be a laugh to give you six choices, as if it's *Who Wants To Be A Millionaire*? Don't they know that you have to get to the end of the six questions before you can work out which one is the right number for you, and then when you do, you've forgotten whether it was number 2 or number 3? When you finally plump for a number without resorting to asking the audience, you get another four choices, and finally you speak to an actual person called Wayne or Dipti, neither of whom can get your details up in front of them because the computers are down.

But the best marketing tactic to assure us we're valued customers was initiated by the financial services industry. When you've been listening to three minutes of Vivaldi repeated twenty times, it's a reassuring touch to be told intermittently **"your call is very important to us."** That's bankers for you. Anyhow, it was customer service and culture which ultimately led us to steady and highly profitable growth and we were getting noticed.

Our first interested buyer was multi-millionaire businessman Nick Gold. I won't bore you with the details of how he got to hear about us. I'd never heard of him but was asked to meet him in his house in North London. I got off the train and was picked up by a chauffeur in a customised Mercedes Benz thing with blacked out windows, cream leather throughout, a coffee machine, two televisions and a champagne fridge.

I wasn't expecting a knackered Fiat Punto, but still it was a bit of a culture shock. When I got to his huge house, I walked past uniformed household staff to our meeting being held in his rather grand but naff bar on the ground floor. He stood on the side of the optics and I sat on a bar stool. Actually, I quite liked him because he was so ridiculous and I think he knew it. From our conversation he was interested enough to arrange a 140-mile round trip visit to our offices for lunch with his 'finance director' to see the operation for himself.

When I got back to the office, me and Brady decided to do a bit of internet stalking on Mr Gold. All we could find was a lot of celebrity gossip columns about the man himself. They gleefully reported on his 2018 wedding to **"former reality tv star"** Laura, the daughter of famous US chef Aldo Zilli and author of the book *High-Class Cooker*, which also happened to be the name of her tv show. Classy. Nick was most often described in these reports as a 'music mogul' and Ms Zilli as a 'beauty'.

The wedding ceremony was conducted on a Florida beach with hundreds of 'society' guests some of whom appeared to be wearing next to nothing. The marriage was sealed with a kiss in front of hordes of photographers. The lovely couple followed that with a London celebration in which Boy George supplied the music. I cannot even imagine how much it all would have cost. There were also lots of other glamorous pictures on Instagram of private yachts, luxury jets and glorious sunsets. How we laughed.

The day of the meeting arrived. As is usual, we never offer up sandwiches for our guests but laid out a nice lunch of salads, cold meats, smoked salmon and beautiful bread. When he arrived, we had a rather bizarre meeting where we went through our finances and business plan, but most importantly our ethos and culture. He didn't listen to anything much we said, neither did his finance guy. He fidgeted a lot, obviously had a very low attention span and would abruptly make phone calls to other people during the meeting in which he was incredibly rude to whoever was on the other end. He swept out of the office from whence he came after two hours.

A couple of days later he offered me an exclusivity deal. He would give me £1 million now to exclusively deal with him about the sale of the company for the next 6 months, while he tracked our profit levels, thought it over and considered a final price offer. His terms were that if he decided not to go ahead, I could keep the money anyhow. It was very obvious to me that he would have started to interfere in what we were doing over the course of that period and therefore the answer was 'no'. Can you imagine our values chiming with the way he speaks to people and our staff remaining in the company even if eventually we didn't sell to him? I would have lost my greatest assets. He could not believe he had been turned down. He said I was unbelievably stupid at passing up £1 million, which I could keep come what may and that I was pretty rubbish at being an entrepreneur. I didn't bother replying.

The next year it was reported that Nick and his father Peter, were accused of conning the Swedish state out of £4.25 million. An investigation by journalists allegedly revealed that they sold 'ice-melting chemicals' to councils which weren't some magical new technology after all. In fact it was 96 percent road salt. The difference being they were sold for 165 times the price of road salt. Then in 2020, less than two years after getting married, Laura filed for divorce because Nick had gone bust owing just over £22 million (£22,038,795.50 to be precise) to a range of creditors. I think I made the right decision.

CHAPTER 14
Swimming lessons

"The elevator to success
is out of order. You'll have to use
the stairs, one step at a time."

Joe Girard

After the Nick Gold episode, I gathered a team to help me sell the business to someone more suitable. I engaged a highly professional business broker, Sian Murray, the fabulous lawyer Susan Jennings and the slightly mad but incredibly intelligent Margaret Connolly who was so good at tax matters I think HMRC named a loophole after her (joke). We set about selling the business to someone who would 'fit' with what we'd created. By coincidence we were an all-female team. No egos in there and along with Brady, we worked together brilliantly.

We had some 37 enquiries from a range of investors, competitors and businesses keen to expand and we considered eight serious offers from buyers we really respected. Eventually, just to make all those critics who've given us a hard time look pretty stupid, the business was sold to EY (Ernst and Young) in early 2020. Quite rightly we went through the most extraordinary forensic due diligence and came out of it all with flying colours because our processes, reporting mechanisms and quality standards are of the highest calibre. They're a multi-billion pound international company who are really keen to implement new types of working cultures and innovative marketing and see if it can be applied to a huge organisation.

Naturally, this is a much trickier challenge than hard-wiring culture into just 20 or so people, but a worthy aim nonetheless. Brady continues to run the company with her usual skill and good humour. In the deal, all our staff were kept on. We absolutely insisted on that. They work in the same office and with the same flexible working hours as before, but as new EY employees they have much more security and a career trajectory that I could never have offered them.

For anyone who is interested in the nuts and bolts of going from zero to selling to a multi-billion pound blue chip in five years, I thought I would list some of the things I learned along the way. Don't forget that aside from these the most important element is people. Recruiting those that have the same values as you and are prepared to thoroughly own your vision is top priority.

On creating a high performing fast growth business

1. Staff always know what the issues are, they may not know how to sort them out, but they know what they are. Most especially those just below the management layer. Make sure you have clear communication lines, and you have a culture where it's ok to articulate problems. If not, you will become removed and isolated from the operational reality and eventually there will be a catastrophic failure which you never saw coming. The issues are almost always people.

Something like the wrong person in the wrong job, unclear about what they're supposed to do or confusion over line management. Clarity is essential. Spell it out and make it very clear what is expected and what success looks like. Don't rush it, be patient and make sure people really understand things at their own pace.

2. Have regular reviews about performance and your reportee's ambitions and make them 360 degree meetings i.e. is your management style hindering them? Or as I always put it to my staff during appraisals **"what is it that I'm doing that drives you mad?"** When they say nothing, the reply is always **"oh come on, there must be something"**, push it and then you can start having great conversations about how to create a workplace that brings

out the best in them. Drop your ego because when you're at the top feedback is a gift that is not given lightly by anyone in your pay.

3. Play to innate behaviour where possible, rather than force behaviour. Of course, everyone has a bit of their job they don't really like, but if it's something they're inherently bad at, it takes a lot of effort to change natural behaviours. We tend to refine the job role instead. We know we'll never get a person who fits a job criteria 100 percent. If they're great at 90 percent of their job, we don't waste time worrying about the other 10 percent and having awful appraisal meetings talking about the bits they're bad at. Look across the company and see who else can pick up on that element, probably someone who loves doing that stuff anyhow. If you play to people's strengths, they will increase in confidence, take less managing and become really productive.

4. Good management should not be done in a noisy dramatic style but in a calm and systematic manner. Follow everything through day after day. Has this been done? Where are we on that? Why are these figures looking different from last month? Make people feel good about what they do but be absolutely, brutally honest if things are not right. You can be kind in the way you do it. But never let anything slip, because it will only come back to bite you, only it will be much bigger and at a time when it's incredibly inconvenient. You can use great care and humour but never shirk the difficult conversations. Being hard in business is about making considered and objective decisions, not being shouty macho when things have gone wrong because you didn't listen or tackle it early enough.

5. Talking of which, spend a lot of time looking and listening. You have to be there and not out and about too

much or shut away in a remote office where you can't observe. Be amongst it as often as you can. Most people want to do a good job and try hard to do so. If that's not happening, then it's probably a failure of the structure or processes and you need to be able to see that first-hand and then work out how to change it. Insist on an open and communicative culture.

If your staff feel they will be blamed for failure, they won't mention problems or identify issues and they'll go to ground so you won't spot them. The more you know about the problems, the more likely you are to be able to sort them out and quickly. This will then involve small, iterative changes and not massive, disruptive change swings which are unsettling for everyone. Speed of change is critical to success especially in making swift moves against the competition.

6. Constantly look for things to remove and simplify. First question when you arrive at your desk every day is why are we doing this? Is there an easier way? What could we be doing instead? We are happy to go through 99 things that don't work to find one that does. Our concept of failure is that it brings us closer to the key thing that does work. If you constantly streamline you will not become a bureaucratic, slow-moving dinosaur.

7. Be even tempered always. You cannot even have one bad day at work. It doesn't matter how bad you feel, every day you have to be right on everything and bright with it. Your people want you to be consistent and even handed. They want you to be decisive but not impetuous and calm in a crisis. When there's a mistake it's your fault, when there's a success it's the team that takes the credit. Everyone is relying on you for their jobs, so in a personal capacity you have to be fresh and energetic every day.

You need to learn to be excellent at time management. So again, at your desk first thing you need to look at all the things you have to do and see if there is anything you can give someone else. If your calendar is booked from 8am to 6pm with no gaps, it's not because you're important or irreplaceable, it's because you're not managing your time properly. Say no to meetings that don't need you. Offer up replacements who can attend if it's not vital you personally need to be there. Make sure that a couple of times a week there are some 2 hour slots that are booked in as 'no appointments'. Brief staff that these cannot be overridden in any circumstances. You must have time to think and breathe and to observe.

8. As mentioned in Chapter 6, the client comes first, always and without question. Too many companies decide how they want to work and then push that onto their clients. They decide a type of payment system is operationally easier but it's not convenient for their customers. They have a process which might make internal admin simpler but annoys customers no end. They sub-contract to a delivery partner who are unreliable but cheap and don't get me started again on call centres. Work out the customer's needs front and centre with all the touchpoints they will have with you, then map out your customer-centric processes, customer-centric marketing and customer-centric service. Happy customers are the best marketing force ever and will drive growth.

9. I get very uneasy around people who describe themselves as a business 'guru' or business 'consultant' but their past track record doesn't really stand scrutiny. Instead of shelling out serious money to see these people who, I'm afraid to say, are generally well past middle age, white and male and not well connected to the massive changes in the business world

in the last five years, find a mentor. Ask someone you admire if they would mind giving you some time once a month or so. Their listening skills and individual advice are gold dust.

10. If you run out of cash your business is dead. This has nothing to do with success or failure. You can have lots of repeat business in the pipeline and new clients coming on board, but cash can still be scarce. Even when growth is flat there is a considerable lag between doing the work and getting paid with overheads needing to be settled immediately. Keeping control of that gap is critical. The most dangerous time for a business is when it grows quickly. The overheads that need paying straight away become bigger but getting paid by clients doesn't always happen at the same pace. The quicker you grow the worse this can get. If necessary, turn down some work in order to grow at the correct speed.

In terms of chasing people who owe you money, you have to have a process that systematically addresses payment. Always follow up on late payers, politely but assertively. Always. If you can't do it, get someone who can. I want to scream when a business owner says they can't chase because a very big order has been placed and they're such an important client. Well, they're not a client if they haven't paid, and they're definitely not an important client if they default.

On developing a marketing strategy

11. Use the behaviour change principles as detailed in Chapter 6 to get customers to buy your services or product. Make sure this is integrated into day-to-day operational marketing and longer-term strategic marketing plans. But, critically it should have only one common goal. A goal or end game that's absolutely clear to you. And that should

not be about creating 'buzz' around your idea or product. Or the number of Twitter followers, LinkedIn connections, website visitors, magazine articles etc. These things are useful and interesting but they're not the point. Some business owners get obsessed with these numbers, but really that's just pure vanity. All of these elements are just steps on the way. Hopefully they're part of a well-conceived, integrated and co-ordinated marketing plan; deliberately and painstakingly put together to achieve the one and only outcome that really matters . . . sales and profitable sales at that. If not, your company will eventually die.

You might have a lifestyle business or a social enterprise or charity, and that's quite different. This could give you endless satisfaction and pleasure without a growth or profit motive and there's nothing wrong with that. But if you want to get big or get bought, every marketing decision (and every business decision actually), should be driven with this end game in mind. So, if you want to generate big profits by selling products via your website, you can deliberately plan to achieve, say 5,000 Twitter followers. But this is only relevant if your type of client uses Twitter anyway, and only if this eventually drives them to your website and they end up buying your product. If Twitter doesn't achieve this for you, then why have you spent time and/or money on it? It will only reduce your overall profitability.

The same can be said of radio advertising, printed publicity, networking. Measure the results of each of the marketing methods you try and hone it down until you find the one/s that result in sales at the end of the day. So, ignore people who say every business must be on social media. Video adverts for incontinence pads aimed at pensioners on TikTok? What do you think?

12. Be a challenger brand that challenges the status quo and questions everything. A challenger brand doesn't occupy the middle ground with all the other also-rans and they don't get to be strong and successful by behaving like a smaller version of the big players. It's the David and Goliath thing; they may be bigger but they're slower and weighed down with establishment expectation, loss aversion, political correctness and historical context. Also, they're complacent.

If you come up against a Goliath with an eight-foot spear, you wouldn't choose a four foot one to fight him with. Which is what business owners do all the time! We can't match their weapons or their strength or size, so we have to choose something different – a stone for example. With the right attitude and confidence and not playing by the rules, we can create our own market of customers who don't really like the big boys anyhow, one where the attitude to customer service is significantly different. And of course, one for which your competitors are wholly unsuited and uncompetitive. That's exactly what we did. Our clients generally hated traditional accountants and so they were keen to try our alternative.

13. As I've said before get yourself a very confident solid identity. Don't offer a wishy washy vision of who you are. Be vivid and salient in the descriptions of your business and service or product. Aim to create an emotionally based rather than a rationally based relationship with your clients. Clients buy services or products with their heart – surprisingly often it is not a rational decision. Emotional products or services are about a strong, distinct, authentic message that tells people why you do what you do, not just what you do.

When you have that nailed it's so hard for others to copy because ultimately you're not offering yet another service or product in that market, you're offering your own personal conviction and unique story. As our name became more well-known and we expanded, we found our clients had an enthusiastic preference for our services and our company. They really liked us because of our authentic identity and of course because we put them at the centre of everything we did. They referred their friends and business associates and that's the best marketing you can get (and the cheapest!).

On selling your business

14. Don't fall in love with your product or service. Everywhere you look, aspiring entrepreneurs are being told to 'do what you love and success will follow'. But suggesting you have to be smitten with your product to succeed is nonsense and bad advice. You need to be passionate about what you do, but dispassionate about your business otherwise you can't make good decisions. I have seen this time and time again with start-ups. An entrepreneur has taken out a loan, begged and borrowed from their families, been on *Dragon's Den*, mortgaged their family home or whatever. All because they're obsessed by their product (or service) idea. But . . . in a bad way, not a good way.

So many times the best advice they could've received right at the beginning is 'don't do it', or at least 'don't sink money into it.' It might be smart, it might be technologically advanced and totally amazing, but the number one question is will anyone want to buy it? Truly want to buy it? Not just like it, and be interested in it, that's not the right question. Make sure you test your ideas; talk to your friends, family and even stop people in the street. The question you must ask them is: **"Would you get your bankcard out now and pay for this incredible thing I have come up with?"** There's only going to be two possible answers.

15. If selling your company is your ultimate game plan, the best path to hyper profitability is to get involved in a fast-growing sector <u>and</u> be all over your numbers. Don't be first to market it's incredibly hard to make it work without huge amounts of investment. Research the markets and sectors that are growing fast and hitch a ride. Then, crucially, be passionate about creating the business culture that will allow creativity and ideas to flow.

It really doesn't matter what the business does; it's about finding expanding sectors, not ones that are crowded with competitors fighting each other. In this scenario, it's a race to the bottom with high volume and low margins and not differentiation. In addition, if you're serious about business you need to get financially literate. Buyers are weighing up value and risk. You must know your cashflow figures, profit and loss and balance sheet details on a daily basis. Watch these like a hawk and make early corrective adjustments before anything becomes a crisis. If you don't understand figures, learn and learn fast. You cannot sell a company if you don't know the fundamentals of finance.

16. Always get the best lawyer, tax accountant and business broker you can find when selling your business. You cannot do this on your own and you need highly skilled and trusted advisers by your side every step of the way. It's a long and gruelling journey. They also need to be experienced enough to tell you when you're views are unrealistic or you're just being a plain idiot.

17. In the final year before you sell you need to be down to working just two or three days a week. First, you need to create the space to go through the due diligence process which takes huge amounts of time. If you don't, you'll be trying to do your day job and run the business and income

will inevitably fall. This puts the buyer in a great position because if revenue drops they can negotiate a lesser sale price.

Secondly, you have to prove the business can run without you, or else what is it that they're buying? They're buying you, not the business. This means that they will need you to stay on, working full time after the sale with tough targets to meet but no influence on how it's run. Is that what you want?

On avoiding people that don't share your values

18. Try and only do business with nice people. It's hard to start with, when sales are difficult to come by and profits have not yet materialised, because you need to grab every client and every opportunity you can. But as we grew and became more financially stable, we wouldn't work with rude or unfairly demanding clients and we could be more picky in our choice of suppliers and business partners. We got to a place where we were in an environment that was almost entirely populated by people who were ethical and shared our ideals.

In other words, avoid dick heads if you can. These are people that talk a good game but leave an awful trail of destruction behind them. When you're faced with someone who seems to be a bully, way too arrogant or just plain rude, check them out. Look on the internet and work out if the claims they make are true and investigate their previous directorships on Companies House. What is their past business history and are there any dodgy stories around? You certainly don't want to get involved with a Simon Horrobin, Nick Gold or Kevin Dougall. All that matters is what they do or have done, not what they say. I think I should have researched and checked out clients and business associates much more thoroughly than I did. Please do this on every occasion such a person presents themselves, it will save a lot of time and money. If after all that research, you still decide to work with them, proceed with caution.

Reputational management

19. Reputational management is the invisible advantage. Track it and measure it if possible. Prospective clients will compare you with your rivals, don't think they don't do this. They do. So, the aim is to gain a reputational 'halo'. Live your values and ethics and make sure you are truly customer-centric and consistently world class at customer service.

The definition of reputation in a business context is client expectation versus experience fulfilment. If you exceed expectation with the service experienced, your reputation is positive. A good reputation enables you to adopt premium pricing and attract and keep top recruits. You will gain greater customer and employee loyalty and achieve stable revenues.

On dealing with the media

20. Don't. Unless you're professionally trained or have no choice.

Following these tenets and learning from my previous stupid mistakes made my company very attractive to buyers. It eventually made me pretty rich by most people's standards. In business, I think if you can survive the first three years using the above principles you are in with a very good chance of outstanding success. But you'll need to be determined, have lots of stamina and persistently march forward despite the barriers. Then with a small amount of luck thrown in, it can be done.

At last, I own my own house again, so no more renting for me. I admit it's a bit posh but why not? I can afford it now. The funny thing is, just before this happened and when I wasn't looking for it, I also got to know the nicest, kindest man I've ever met. He's handsome and talented, witty and well-read and has no desire to ever be the centre of attention. I love him very deeply but this time it's a different love. It's uncomplicated and soft, completely accepting of who we both are and entirely mutual on all levels. I feel so safe in the knowledge that it isn't about power or abuse and I know exactly what to expect when I come home and open the front door . . . a warm hug and the kettle on, exactly the same as the day before and the one before that.

We quietly got married with just two witnesses in the autumn of 2021. It was in a railway station car park on a rainy Monday and Simon (temporarily) lost the ring. I'm not joking. Afterwards we went on our own for a jolly nice lunch in a local pub and it was everything we wanted it to be.

To top it all I was awarded a CBE in the New Year Honours list of 2022, for services to small businesses. That was a bit of a surprise, I thought the letter from the Cabinet Office was because I'd done something wrong again! As my lovely aunty Marjorie said, who is now 87 and used to sleep in the same bed with her three sisters, "that's not supposed to happen to people like us." Well, it has and it can. I've managed to do this, so if you're bloody minded enough, you can too. But I'll only wish you good luck if you're prepared to do it with humanist kindness.

Tom Daley also got a gong at the same time. He's only 27 years old, but I was so impressed by what he said:

"Accepting an OBE is one thing but accepting it and doing something with it (is another). I feel it's really important to lift up all the people who feel like they're outsiders and don't fit in and feel like they have been 'less than' for so many years – to support them in being what they want to be."

A superb response and it made me think, that I too, need to leverage it to reach out and help more people find their voices and help make bullying and discrimination ever more unacceptable.

Finally, most evenings, in a neat twist of fate, I follow my old routine and get ready to go swimming. Now, it really is in my very own heated outdoor pool in the grounds of our recently acquired home. And as I do so, I take a quick backward glance at the newly painted outside toilet conveniently built some ten yards away. I think of all those people that have tried to undermine, ignore, harass, or intimidate me and I allow myself a wry smile.

DEAR READER

If you too believe that kindness and equality is the way forward in business (and life!), please do pass this book on to your friends and colleagues. It's also available for just £1 on Kindle and is free as an audiobook via Spotify, Audible, Podbean etc.

www.susiews.com

ACKNOWLEDGEMENTS

In order to make sure I don't laze about too much now I've sort of retired, I try to keep 'sending the elevator down' as they would say in the USA. To this end, I still run and personally fund a radio programme called *The FoodTalk Show.* It started in 2016 and I've recorded these programmes with amazing guests every week since then and now have a collection of over 300 podcasts on spotify, audible, on podcast apps and via syndicated radio stations. To me, this is an important charitable venture to highlight and promote the incredible work of local food and drink producers, our growers, farmers and hospitality venues. We need to support local family businesses, value food security and celebrate the people who are guardians of our fields and woodlands, and this is my bit to help.

Below are some messages to the businesswomen I have had the pleasure to meet and/or work with over the last couple of years. Many have been via *The FoodTalk Show* and other radio programmes and podcasts I've hosted but also through some of my charitable or work-related ventures. Although I'm wary of the mainstream media as the infamous Arse Lady, at least if I host radio programmes or co-host podcasts I can edit out any catastrophic errors!

I have too many good friends to mention who have helped me through some bleak times, not least the 'Portugal' trio of Julia Witz, Sue Last and Carolyn Bird (who btw has also helped me so much with my research projects). Thank you to you all. You may not know it, but you've all been an inspiration one way or another. Worthy of a special citation are . . .

• **Suki Fuller**, deservedly on the *Black Powerlist Titans of Tech* and Tech Nation's *50 Most Inspiring and Influential Black Voices* – you might be sought after for your experience in the early adoption of emergent technologies but really you and me just like a good lunch.

• **Jacquie Davis**, the world's top female bodyguard and inspiration for the Netflix film *Close* – I've never met anyone so fearless as you. You've been stabbed, shot at several times, chased through some of the world's most dangerous countries and rescued men imprisoned by Saddam Hussein's son, Uday, in Iraq. You're extraordinary and remind me not to moan about the small stuff.

• **Dr Sue Black OBE**, Professor of Computer Science and saviour of Bletchley Park – a great fellow speaker and proof that starting in a women's refuge with three young children need not be a barrier to success.

• **Asma Kahn**, owner of Darjeeling Express, star of Netflix's *Chef's Table* and true lover of London – you inspire me to be more 'feisty', and I hope I will have the honour of interviewing you again for *The FoodTalk Show*.

• **Dr Gail Louw**, one of our best and most courageous modern playwrights – our trip to Berlin to watch your play about a Hitler sympathiser was pretty scary. Can we do something less controversial next time?

• **Hari Ghotra**, founder of the biggest digital Indian food platform in the UK – I still dream about your tomato-based red lentil dahl.

• **Sheila Dillon**, one of six women who successfully brought a landmark sex discrimination case in the US for equal pay in the 1960s. An investigative food journalist and presenter of *Radio 4's The Food Programme* – our paths cross periodically, and I know you'll be embarrassed by this, but you're a personal heroine of mine.

• **Floortje Hoette**, CEO of Produced in Kent and passionate advocate for local food – I promise we'll get more support for our county's wonderful food and drink producers.

• **Jan Hawkins**, HR Director at Westinghouse (retired) and my favourite American buddy – when can we meet up in the US again and pretend to ourselves that we're cool hippy beach bums?

• **Stephanie Karpetas OBE**, Department for Business, Energy and Industrial Strategy and sustainability champion – striking out on your own with two-year-old twins made me realise that I could achieve things without a partner too.

- **Dr Heather Heathfield**, formerly Director for Innovation and Insight at the British Red Cross – we worked on some amazing health projects using ground-breaking research methodology, but to me your ability to drink wine while apparently not having eaten anything much for days is another of your skills.
- **Barbara Cooper**, KCC's former Director of Growth, Environment and Transport, a department with over a thousand employees and a multi-gazillion pound budget – a great example of a good person who carried out their hugely difficult role with skill, pragmatism, patience and a fab sense of humour.
- **Hilary Meredith**, Professor of Law and Freeman of the City of London – our husbands (before we left them) were the barbecue brothers and we clung to each other when we were trying to have a career, study and bring up children, but only you could've ended up marrying David Beckham's dad.
- **Kumud Ghandi**, food scientist and spice expert, famed for cooking for clients as diverse as Nelson Mandela and Madonna – you are one of my best-loved co-presenters on *The FoodTalk Show* and one of the most knowledgeable.
- **Renée Elliott**, no-nonsense pioneer founder and former CEO of Planet Organic – a fellow *Future Food Awards* judge and a great example of how to spot a gap in the market and go for it.
- **Somi Arian**, founder of FemPeak, award-winning film maker and retired rock star – my sort of adopted daughter, I think we make a great broadcasting duo a bit like a podcast version of Morecambe & Wise, although coming from a small town outside Tehran I doubt you'll understand the cultural reference!
- **Roxane Naro Markarian**, an impressively qualified research engineer and partner at EY - proud to leave my company in your capable hands.
- **Sarah Luxford**, one of the *Top 10 Most Influential Women in UK Tech* and Partner at Gatenby Sanderson – you have the most contagious laugh ever and you've quietly done more to get UK women into tech than almost anyone I can think of.
- **Dr Roma Patel**, superb healthcare professional and a great neighbour - please don't bring toffee vodka around my house anymore.
- **Susannah Schofield OBE**, DSA Director General amongst other things and the wonderful **Deborah Turner**, The FSB National Lead for Women in Enterprise – Schofield and Turner, the double act that never fails to make me laugh so much I can barely breathe.

- **Pinky (Nusrat Mehboob) Lilani CBE**, fierce advocate and supporter of women in business – one of my favourite food memories was at your beautiful home discussing rum babas, while eating your lovingly prepared food. As you say "coriander makes all the difference."
- **Dame Stephanie Shirley DBE, CH**, the first female tech pioneer in the UK, astounding businesswoman and generous philanthropist arriving in the UK, fleeing the nazis as an unaccompanied Jewish child refugee aged five – a true role model even some 60 years later, our joint podcast with Somi Arian (above) was a real honour.
- **Maggie Philbin OBE**, *Tomorrow's World* and *Swap Shop* tv presenter and broadcaster – another fabulous radio interviewee where we got to chat for a whole hour about your work as founder and CEO of TeenTech which reaches some 12,000 young people every year. Every Saturday a very long time ago you were part of my childhood!

And last, but absolutely by no means least:
- **Brady Last**, the magnificent MD of EY Breakthrough Incentives (formerly Breakthrough Funding) and Associate Partner at EY - couldn't have done it without you babe and never forget how bloody brilliant you are. Ever.

Justice rally, Melbourne

'Defining our future' protesters, Toronto

Printed in Great Britain
by Amazon

13777071R00136